THE
Knack
OF
Selling
Yourself

C000231152

JAMES T. MANGAN

THE DARTNELL CORPORATION
CHICAGO · NEW YORK · LONDON

Also by the Same Author

YOU CAN DO ANYTHING

THOUGHTS ON SALESMANSHIP

PUSH

LEARN TO WRITE

DESIGN—THE NEW GRAMMAR OF ADVERTISING

REVISED AND ENLARGED EDITION

First Printing, December 1938
Second Printing, February 1939
Third Printing, May 1939
Fourth Printing, October 1939
Fifth Printing, April 1940
Sixth Printing, January 1942
Seventh Printing, June 1947

Contents

The Knack of Selling Yourself

Introduction

SECTION 1

Expression

SPEAKING   *Page*

1. Speak Up! 34
2. Speak Correctly 36
3. Learn Conversation 38

   Avoid Facts 38

4. Become a Public Speaker 39

   The First Rule 40
   Loudly and Clearly 40
   Admit No Weakness 41
   Do Something Positive 41
   Avoid the Mike 41
   Go in Empty 42
   How You Say It 42
   Concentrate 43

CONTENTS

WRITING   *Page*

  1. Write! 44
  2. Write in Volume 45
  3. Toot Your Own Horn 46

ACTING

  1. Put on a Front and Get Away with It! 48

     Gamble on Good Clothes 49
     Posture Makes "That Handsome Male" 50
     Think of Someone Who's Very Straight . . . 51
     Think of Someone Who's Very Stooped . . . 52
     Come "Clean"! 52

  2. Show Some Spirit! 53

     Concentrate with Zip and Emphasis! 54
     Personality—Child of Spirit 54
     Cultivate That Radical Streak 55

  3. Be an Egotist—and Make Them Like It! . . . 56
     That Small Idea You Have of Yourself . . . 57

  4. Enthusiasm—the Quality That Never Fails . . . 58

     Turn It On! 59
     Listen to the Sound of Your Own Voice . . . 59
     See That You Yourself Are Sold 60
     Boost 61
     Associate with Enthusiastic People 61
     Have a Goal—Reach It! 62
     Slice Off a Piece of the Future 62
     From the Inside Out! 62
     Ignore the Handicaps 63
     Faster! Faster! 64
     Be a Child Again 64

CONTENTS

CREATING   *Page*

   1. Invent Things, Invent Ideas 65
   2. Steal from the Clock—and Produce 67

      Go on a "Work Bender" 69

SECTION 2

Promise

   1. Talk of Tomorrow 72
   2. Pass the White Meat 74
   3. Don't Let Them Pin a Label on You 76
   4. Why People Marry 78
   5. Hand Out the "Dream Stuff" 80
   6. "No Imagination?" How Sad! 81
   7. Stay Young the Rest of Your Life 83
   8. Grow—and You Click! 85
   9. Say "Yes" Without Your Tongue in Your Cheek . 86
 10. Never Say "No" 87
 11. Always Have Good Intentions 87
 12. The Best Way to Create Promise Is Not to Promise
      at All 88
 13. Be a "Bear for Work" 88
 14. Throw Away Your Hammer and Get a Horn . . . 89

SECTION 3

Guts

   1. Carry a Punch and Use It 93
   2. Don't Ask the Boss if It's All Right with Him . . 94
   3. The Slave Driver's Touch 96
      Be Bold "Out Loud" 97

GUTS—CONTINUED   *Page*

  4. Stand on Your Own Feet 97
  5. "Ignorant Nerve" Comes in Handy 99
  6. "I'm Going Home for Supper with Ma and Pa!" . 100
  7. "I Saw Him First!" 101
  8. Stick to Your Guns 102
  9. Always Carry a Bank Roll 105
10. Rise to Your Full Height 106
11. The Other Man Is Just as Scared as You Are. . . 107
12. They Don't Care About You 107
13. You Have Only One Person to Account to . . . 110

SECTION 4

Approach

1. Connections 114
2. If You Would Percolate, Circulate!. 116
3. The List to Which You Send Christmas Cards . . 117
4. Be Nice to His Secretary. 118
5. Never Resist the Buyer Who Wants to Do You a
    Favor 119
6. Start a Bank Account of New Friends and
    Acquaintances 120
7. Keep Up with Your Old Friends and Acquaintances 123
8. The Better the Connection, the Less You
    Should Use It 124

TEN TIPS ON APPROACH

1. Develop an "Approach Personality" 125
2. Make a List 125
3. Get a Reputation 125

CONTENTS

TEN TIPS ON APPROACH—CONTINUED   *Page*

   4. Hire the Best Talent 125
   5. Write Plenty of Letters 126
   6. Study the Approach Methods of Others 126
   7. Put Yourself in the Shoes of the Man You're
       Trying to Approach 126
   8. Know the Big Shots 126
   9. Any Contact Is a Good Contact 127
  10. Learn How to Go Over a Man's Head 127

SECTION 5

Diplomacy

VISIBLE DIPLOMACY

   1. When He Bores You with a Long-Winded Story . . 130
   2. Are You a Little Bit "Off"? 130
   3. Secrets of a Good Mixer 131
      Let People Know You're Glad to See Them . . . 133
   4. Marks of a Good Yes-Man 134
   5. Are You Too Cheap? 136
   6. Legitimate Bribery 137
   7. Pay Your Debt Before It's Due. 140
   8. Go Out of Your Way to Be Nice 140
   9. Left-Handed Compliments Are Always Good . . . 141
  10. Leave a Good Taste in Their Mouths 142
  11. Avoid the Open Break 142

INVISIBLE DIPLOMACY

   1. Don't Say What You Think! 144
   2. Play Politics to a Fare-Thee-Well 146

CONTENTS

INVISIBLE DIPLOMACY—CONTINUED   *Page*

  3. Your Private Brand Should Copy the "Big Time"
     Variety 148
  4. Nothing Is Sacred in Politics—Except Gratitude . 150
  5. Losing Ground to Gain Ground 151
  6. "Leave Him with a Smile": A Hint to Employees
     and Employers 152

SECTION 6

Familiarity

  1. What Kind of Buddy Are You? 156
  2. Make Your Hobbies Pay Dividends 158
  3. Be Yourself 160
  4. Cultivate the Universal Streak 165
  5. Be Sympathetic! 166
  6. "High-Keyed" Generally Means "High-Salaried" . 168
  7. Call Him by His First Name 171
  8. Does Familiarity Breed Contempt?. 173

SECTION 7

Reliability

CHARACTER

  1. The Anchor of Your Personality 176
  2. You Must Not Be "Two-Faced" 177
  3. Tell the Truth 178
  4. Keep Your Promises 179
  5. Build Good Health 180
  6. Grade Up! 181

CONTENTS

ABILITY   *Page*

    1. How's Your Grey Matter? 183
    2. Cut Out the Red Tape 185
    3. Don't Say "I Think" 186
    4. Remember? 187
    5. Move in Faster Company 190
    6. The Source of All Ability—Straight Thinking. . 193
    7. Logic 193
    8. The Cultivation of Ability 200

CONSERVATIVENESS

    1. The Trick of Understatement 200
    2. Think Before You Answer 202

SELF-CONFIDENCE

    1. Sell Yourself to Yourself 203
    2. That "Air of Assurance" 205

SECTION 8

Persuasiveness

DIRECT PERSUASIVENESS

    1. "High Pressure" 209
    2. Getting Others Involved in Your Projects . . . 210
    3. Make Yourself Indispensable to the "Boss" . . . 212
    4. Ask 214
    5. Get the Name on the Dotted Line 215
    6. Use the Deadline 215
    7. The Value of Making a Nuisance Out of Yourself 216

CONTENTS

INDIRECT PERSUASIVENESS   *Page*

   1. The Six Ancient Foes of Persuasion 218

      Suspicion 218
      Inertia 219
      Fear 219
      Pride 220
      Incompetency 220
      Jealousy 221

   2. Find the Angle and Speed the Sale 221
   3. Reach Home with a Real Jolt 222
   4. The Larceny Motive—Something for Nothing . . 223
   5. The Greed Motive—Grab It, Mister! 224
   6. The Motive of Self-Interest—Me and Mine . . 224
   7. The Vanity Motive—Everybody's a Show-Off . 225
   8. The Self-Preservation Motive—Save Me! . . . 226
   9. The Reproduction Motive—the Proud Daddy . . 226
  10. The Convenience Motive—the Big Loafer! . . 227
  11. The Appeal to Pleasure—Ain't We Got Fun? . . 227
  12. The Bow to Laziness 228
  13. The Self-Development Motive 229
  14. "Under Cover" Is Better than "Out in the Open" . 230
  15. The Invisible Art of Suggestion 233

THE RELATIVE IMPORTANCE OF EACH QUALITY . . 237

Do Something About It

YOU'RE REALLY WORTH IT! 246

YOU'RE ONLY JUST STARTING 248

MAKE A MANIFESTO! 250

GO INTO ACTION TODAY! 252

Aftermath

Page

AN APPLE FOR THE TEACHER? 258

AUTHOR WANTS TO MAKE MILLION QUICK 259

NOTE ON RELIABILITY 260

WRITE A BOOK 261

THE 25 BEST SOLD "MEN" 262

SOMETHING INTERESTING TO SAY 264

GEORGE STILL DOES IT! 265

A MAGAZINE READER 266

A BUSINESS WRITER 267

A SCHOOLTEACHER 270

A COPYWRITER 271

A PROMOTION MAN 272

A CLERK 273

MORE ON LOGIC

    Calling It Logic Doesn't Make It Logic 274
    Starting Out with the Conclusion 275
    Putting Into Your Mouth Words You Never Said . . . 276
    Laugh It Off 277
    On Whose Authority? 277
    The Question! 278
    Giving a Detail the Importance of an Essential 278
    Is Another, and Opposite, Conclusion Possible? 280
    Do You Know Any More Than You Knew in the Beginning? 280
    Count the Noses! 280
    Spirit Is Not Proof 281
    Logic Is Law—Logic Is Not Man 282

CONTENTS

ABOUT ALWAYS CARRYING $50   *Page*

A POLICE SERGEANT 283

A MAGAZINE PUBLISHER 283

A MULTIMILLIONAIRE 284

A SALESMAN 285

CHANGE FOR TWENTY 285

DEAR OLD COLLEGE CHUM 287

DEAR BRANCH MANAGER 288

DEAR AUDITOR 289

DEAR LAWYER 290

QUESTIONS AND ANSWERS 290

TIP ON SHOWMANSHIP 295

BEFORE PERSUADING—STUDY YOUR MAN! 297

DEFINITION OF "A REGULAR FELLOW" 304

SUNDAY SCHOOL SERMON 304

LETTERS 306

ADDITIONAL THOUGHTS ON PUBLIC SPEAKING . . . 309

PROMISE NEVER SUBMITS TO A SHOWDOWN 315

MORE LETTERS 316

The Knack of Selling Yourself

BY JAMES T. MANGAN

☆

INTRODUCTION

A New Kind of Hard Work

The ideas and propositions in this book are going to disturb many people who will slam the covers shut in disgust, turn their backs and call the author many miserable names. I'm thinking of the hundreds of conversations I've had in which, swinging over to the subject of how to sell yourself, I've been rash enough to advance some of these findings. People who are highly conscious of their own character and righteousness always feel insulted and want to leave the room. They refuse to listen, they want no part of these "radical" theories. They, themselves, in the act of getting to their positions of influence in the world may have faithfully followed all the rules for selling themselves over a whole lifetime, but they will still insist on kidding themselves in their belief they got where they are through ability, character, and hard work.

The whole trouble lies in their failure to distinguish between character and expediency. A man can do an efficient thing, an expedient thing, and not in any way lose or lessen his character. The expediency I urge here is in no way immoral, or even unmoral; though I'll admit it does sound a little irregular in spots simply be-

cause the copy book maxims of morality are so deeply ingrained in all of us.

As I point out in one of the chapters, the essence of all character is CONSISTENCY, *and the most consistent man in the world is he who uses the most direct and efficient means of attaining his goal.*

If your goal is to sell yourself, if you recognize the urgent need and the tremendous value to you which comes from selling yourself, I can assure you that every means set down here is absolutely legitimate. There may be better, that is more apparently virtuous, means for attaining success in life or in your chosen work, but then this is not a book about success, it is a book about how to sell yourself. And when you finally set your heart on selling yourself, you will have to come around to these exact methods. When you do, don't blame the book, don't blame the author; blame the world. I didn't make up these rules, I simply set them down.

And please don't judge this book as a document of human kindness, don't look for sweetness and light in this book. This is not a "How to Win Friends" kind of book; it is not a personal book at all. It attacks the problems of selling yourself in an objective light; it treats ways and means as simple instruments of science. In some cases, therefore, I don't stop to justify the act, that is to moralize or rationalize it, and a certain harshness results which some human beings, still remaining emotional instead of being scientific in the matter, are quick to resent.

And though I offer certain formulas that break with

convention, with the honored counsel of your parents and teachers (all for the sake of achieving a new, a worthy, and a practical goal), there is one point on which I refuse to plead guilty: THIS IS NOT A SHORT-CUT BOOK, THIS IS NOT A BOOK FOR LOAFERS! *I classify reliability, ability, application (work) as seventh in importance in a list of eight necessary qualities, but at no time do I urge that to sell yourself you don't have to work hard.*

As a matter of fact, in acquiring the ability to sell yourself YOU ARE GOING TO HAVE TO WORK HARDER THAN YOU EVER WORKED IN ALL YOUR LIFE. *You are going to have to remake your life along certain lines, acquiring new characteristics and faculties from a scratch start. You are going to have to practice at things to which you are not accustomed and to which you are not instinctively drawn; and yet, if you will turn the drive, the sweat and the patient hours into these exercises and practices, you will come out of it a better and a stronger man. I simply take your nose away from one grindstone and put it up against another grindstone; the new grindstone is a whole lot different from the old but it is an honest-to-goodness grindstone just the same!*

For instance, you are going to have to become a finished public speaker. You are not just going to admit that public speaking ability is a good thing, you are actually going to become a real public speaker, or you can never pass as a man who has sold himself. Do you think that is easy? Do you think it can be done overnight?

Also, you will have to become a writer, a bona fide

writer, who according to Walter Pitkin's definition is a man who has written at least ONE MILLION WORDS. *Do you think that is easy? Do you think it can be done without hard work? Every other single precept in this book centers around a certain talent or ability which you must acquire before you can completely sell yourself.* NOT A SINGLE ONE OF THESE ABILITIES *can be acquired without a fight, a death struggle, and a whole ocean of sweat and application.*

Selling oneself is not a lazy man's game. Most of those who back away from it try to pass the idea off as trivial and not worthwhile, but deep down in their hearts they realize that it is TOO MUCH WORK *for them now. But if* YOU *are not afraid of work, and will agree to put this work into the correct scientific channels, I will promise you sincerely that this book will help you become a man who knows how to sell himself.*

Do You Have to Be Born to It?

Do you have to be disposed by nature toward selling yourself? Must you be son to a father who was a leader, a salesman, a showman?

Not at all! Of course, as you contemplate all that selling yourself requires you will insist you can't make a go of it, because you are timid, or bashful, or afraid of people, or too uneducated to get out into the limelight. You will say that a person has to be born to it to live that way.

But you will be wrong! For the knack of selling yourself is an acquired skill, better and more potent in the possession of the man who has come by it artificially, than in the hands of the man born with it. Most of the men we know who have sold themselves brilliantly have suffered from the same inferior feelings as you. Many great self-salesmen have been woefully under-educated, but the prominence given them in their campaign of selling themselves forced a strong and workable education on them.

You never can tell what you are going to turn out to be once you decide to sell yourself. Every man makes his first speech, writes his first article, engineers his first publicity some time. Once he feels the magic of the first maneuver he becomes a new man, indeed. His very first move at selling himself discloses a whole new world of knowledge to him. His brain starts buzzing like a mighty motor at the revelation. One act of self-promotion immediately begets a dozen more.

Take publicity, for instance. Nobody is born with a flair for publicity; it is strictly an acquired thing. Plan a stroke of publicity, a small or a large maneuver, for yourself. The experiment may fail to click in just the way you desired, but it succeeds in making you an expert. You immediately have some theories about what works in publicity and what misses. New experiments are suggested; pretty soon you are in deep, and by this time several of the experiments have already begun to click!

Any man can be a publicity man if he just works at

it. Any man can be a public speaker, a writer, a leader or organizer if he just works at it. Nor do you have to be young to acquire the new skill. As a matter of fact, middle-aged people, even old folks, who adopt the rational, artificial attitude toward selling themselves can get there even faster than younger people. Their faculty of perspective helps them learn artificial things of a personal nature faster than youth which unconsciously relies more on nature than on reason or skill.

If you will—in a wild dream in your own behalf— ADMIT *that you would like to sell yourself, though you're now convinced you're not born to it, forget your inhibitions, as an experiment, and decide to dabble a little. Just a little! Don't decide to make a big speech—but get up in a public meeting and ask ONE, just one, little question. Don't decide, right off, to write a book—but sit down and pen a short and sensible letter to the Voice of the People column of your newspaper.*

Take it slow, take it easy! Watch it grow—you don't have to be born with it!

Is It Worth the Effort?

Sure it's worth the effort to be able to sell yourself! To feel bold and brave and strong in any company! To have the power of leadership over people, knowing they will work for your cause, respect your inportance, defer to you! It's less miserable to live in the LIMELIGHT *than in a cocoon of introspection and self-conscious* NOTHING-

24

NESS. *Your character is strengthened, your personal virtues enhanced, when they are good enough to stand out in a man with the eyes of the world on him.*

This skill you now have in your chosen profession—who knows you have it besides yourself? How much more valuable would it be if EVERYONE *knew you had this skill, respected you for it, gave you the chance to use it more widely and to pass much of it on to hundreds or thousands of other people! You don't lose character, or skill, or ability by learning to sell yourself. Rather you get the new opportunity of extending these virtues over a much wider sphere!*

Will you look ridiculous if you start to sell yourself? No! Selling yourself is an act of ambition. And the world doesn't scoff at ambitious people—they are all too rare today.

And you needn't fear that your close friends will be shocked at your change. The process is not a fast one; each act of self-promotion is self-strengthening; as you come out of your shell and start changing into a new man, you automatically develop the new strength and poise to support the new you.

It's worth a try—don't be so foolish as to tell yourself it's impossible without a fair try. Make the try and watch the miracle work!

JAMES T. MANGAN

January 1, 1947
Chicago, Ill.

25

☆

The Knack of
Selling Yourself

At school they taught you everything—except the thing
you most needed to know.

They gave you knowledge, training in special abilities, even suggested how you might get ahead in a profession or in business. All the while, from first grade
up, the inference was: If you study and learn, *if you
develop character, practice honesty, and* WORK HARD,
you simply can't fail to make good.

At school they taught you the Merit System. That's
the system that claims the world rewards you according
to how much ability you have and how hard you work.

But alas! your school, my school, and all schools are
wrong about that. The world rewards you not according to how capable you are, but *how well you sell yourself.*

Millions of human beings have kicks coming about

27

the world and the way it's run. In every shop, in every office, in every profession and field of endeavor, the people at the top—those who get the big salaries, and the lion's share of the glory—*are not the ones who know the most.* Dozens of their subordinates may have more real ability than they. But the men at the top *get themselves across* in a loud and positive way, while those with ability to burn let that ability burn up in an internal fire. It never gets out so the world can see it.

Stop and be fair! Perhaps right now, in the place you work, you are jealous of a certain individual who has earned the title, "big shot." Down in your heart you know he's not as smart as you, doesn't deliver as much to the firm as you do, yet he gets the big rewards.

You are judging that man wrongly! He may not be as smart as you according to the Merit System—but then, the Merit System is just a moth-eaten old thing that never got outside of the classroom. He's much smarter than you according to the Get-There System, which is the knack of selling himself, and that's the only system on which the world pays off.

Why squawk because your teachers, with their traditional, old-fashioned precepts, fooled you? Squawking gets you nowhere, it only makes you feel worse. Why not accept the inevitable, adjust your tactics to the world in which you live, and for the sake of the cream you want so badly, *why not learn how to sell yourself?* It's the thing you most need to know!

Selling yourself is an acquired ability, one that could profitably be taught in *every* school, since it is so much needed by individuals out in the world. Selling your-self is the knack of *becoming an important personage, a* SOMEBODY. When you sell yourself, you sell living mer-chandise, and live people buy you, that is, they accord you a place of importance in their hearts and minds. They may like you, love you, desire to give you money, promotion, fame, and even immortality. On the other hand, they may even hate you, want to destroy you. Or they may neither like you nor dislike you—only when a point is made of it, they simply write you down as an important personage. That, in the end, is what selling yourself amounts to: *you make yourself important* to people singly, in groups, or in the public mass.

The principles for selling yourself can be isolated, recorded and offered to you in quite the same way as the rules of arithmetic or grammar. It is our aim to give you these rules here, to hand you a sort of textbook of practical life; the tricks, artifices and schemes of per-sonal action, the magical personal qualities, which secure your worldly objectives. Selling yourself doesn't neces-sarily guarantee that you will make a lot of money, but most people who sell themselves do make money. The thing it does guarantee is that you will have a gay old time leading people, swaying people, basking in their admiration, knowing that you are alive and effec-tive in a world where most humans are impotent and unnoticed.

If it were ever necessary to learn how to sell your-self it's necessary now. The streets are getting wider, as a result of the sidewalks being made narrower. The individual is being pushed back into his shell in behalf of the great impersonal "public welfare." It takes a good man to cross those wide streets without being run down by the roaring traffic. But to the individual who transforms himself into a Get-There specialist, no street is too wide, no crossing too dangerous, to prevent him from reaching his goal.

There are only eight qualities you need to be able to sell yourself. They are:

1. EXPRESSION

2. PROMISE

3. GUTS

4. APPROACH

5. DIPLOMACY

6. FAMILIARITY

7. RELIABILITY

8. PERSUASIVENESS

These qualities are listed in their order of importance and in the chronological order in which you should go about acquiring them. Please observe that the only concession we make to the Merit System is the quality of Reliability, which is listed seventh. There are six other, and more important, qualities you are to acquire, before you take up Reliability.

Don't keep Merit or Reliability as the standard of comparison or it may destroy your perspective. Remember, you are going about this thing scientifically. You are going to sell yourself because *you want to sell yourself*. You are not, in *this* school, seeking to be noble, saintly, or perfect. You are simply out to sell yourself, following the laws which all other important people have followed in order to get there. Isn't that what you're after? The objective may not be ideal, but the knack is real, and the results are marvelous. Let's start the experiment!

☆

___

Expression

For every *impression* you make on another there must have been some *expression* on your part.

Expression consists in taking everything that is inside you—your spirit, your emotion, your intelligence, and all the rest of your ability—and seeing that it definitely gets *outside you,* to reach as large a number of people as possible.

You may be loaded with talent, but it isn't worth two cents until you are able to let others know you have it. When you are out to sell yourself, people are your market. Expression is your means of bringing your goods to market. Analyze the lives of all the great men of history and you'll find that the one quality every one of them excelled in was expression.

And if you were only allowed to have ONE quality with which to sell yourself to others, it would have to be

33

expression. Express yourself! Many times you have
heard, perhaps you have said, these words: "Gee! How
I wish I could express myself!" You were then thinking
of expression as the ability to speak. But expression is
much more than the ability to speak. Edison expressed
himself in invention. Shakespeare expressed himself in
his writing. And perhaps the greatest single feat of
human expression was Lindbergh's flight across the
Atlantic.

Whether *speaking, writing, acting or creating,* expression is simply the ability to make an impression.
Unseen, unheard, and unfelt, you cease to be an individual. To get yourself across today's wide streets, you
simply must learn expression.

Speaking

1. SPEAK UP!

You've sat in on many a conference.

Ever notice how two or three people do all the talking at the conference, how some say absolutely not a
word at all, and how others just murmur a little every
now and then?

The two or three men who do all the talking are
generally the leaders, the ones who guide the decisions
of the conference, THEY SELL THEMSELVES AND THEIR
OWN IDEAS.

Now the people who keep still may have better judgment, experience and ideas than the talkers. But their good judgment and their fine ideas go unused simply because they haven't uncovered them.

Speak up! If you're sitting in on a conference, just don't sit. Say something. Say something as often as you can. The floor belongs to the man who claims it, and the man who speaks is the man whose personality dominates.

Of course, you may say: "It's all right to speak if you have something to say; but why talk and expose my ignorance?" This is foolish reasoning. Analyze what the eager talkers are saying and you'll find they are not saying much at all; you can easily match their intelligence. Then match their aggressiveness and speak up! There would hardly ever be a conference or a meeting if everyone held his tongue until he had something worth while to say.

Speak up! Be heard from no matter where you are. If you attend a public meeting, even if you're a complete stranger in the gathering, *speak up!* Contribute your own individual opinion and ideas! That's the quickest way to let the others know you're alive.

You've been at many a meeting where the floor was thrown open for general discussion and questions, and you had many pertinent things on your mind that you *almost* said. But you just missed speaking up. You were afraid that your voice wouldn't be loud enough, that the people wouldn't stop to notice you, that what you might say would be ridiculed. A mistake, a serious mistake! Never attend a meeting without being an active number in the meeting. A meeting is a great place to get some

35

free advertising for yourself — this advertising is extremely useful in selling yourself, so get the advertising!

By speaking up, you may be elected to office, put on some committee, given some work to do. Don't argue that this is undesirable—it's very, very important in selling yourself. Get on the committee, take the office, and throw in the full force of your personality—the first step in becoming a big-shot.

Speak up! Forget all the old maxims that suggest silence, reserve, and caution. Speak up! Step into the spotlight!

2. SPEAK CORRECTLY

The very best masters of expression—the world's best singers, actors and orators—spend a considerable amount of time every day in voice exercises.

Now if the pro admits the voice is important and, having a good voice, still practices at making it better, how much more so should the amateur recognize its importance!

Though you needn't bring voice cultivation down to a science, you must see to this one all important thing: *that your voice is not muffled.*

It may not be impossible for the man with a muffled voice to sell himself, but it is very, very difficult. Look at all your leaders, look around you where you are working and listen to the heads of the departments, or anyone who enjoys what is known as a good position. You'll find very few muffled voices among executives! They speak sharply and incisively; with their noses, their teeth, their tongues, and their lips.

Their words are not stuck in their throats or imprisoned in their mouths; they are spoken right into the air where they can strike their hearers with the best impact.

Get your voice out of your throat, out of your mouth and into the air! Practice by reading out loud and working the *lips,* the *tongue,* and the *teeth* with exaggerated exactness. Pay attention to your ordinary conversation; use your lips, your tongue and your teeth constantly, and get your words away from your throat.

Important as is the *sound* of your words, of equal importance is the *form* of your words. Speak correctly! The correct speaker is the careful speaker. Take care to keep your sentences in form, to finish every sentence you start, to use perfect grammar, and to have a vocabulary that is strictly appropriate. A big vocabulary, a comprehensive vocabulary, is absolutely worthless, unless you have mastered the meaning of every word and are able to use it with a fine sympathy for patness and expression.

One word used in a poor construction, or a big word used where a short word would have been better, will spoil any speaking performance at once. The guiding principles of good speech are *formality* and *appropriateness.* Think clearly; say what you think; and take the time to say it with exactness, fullness, and perfect form. Concentrate on your form and then all your speaking becomes *practice,* pointing toward perfection.

37

3. LEARN CONVERSATION

Learn to converse as a rational being should converse.
Don't just use the property of speech as a vehicle for
gossip or pastime.

There are few things so rare—and so inspiring—as
good conversation. Only intelligent people know how
to converse properly, and conversation is only useful as
a means of expressing yourself when you have mastered
its fine points.

When two ordinary people meet, what's the first
thing they speak of? The weather! Why? It's common
ground—about the only subject that one is sure the
other knows!

But good conversationalists are never at the mercy
of any particular subject or experience; they are masters of their material and can change from one field to
another without a moment's hesitation. The key to their
conversational art rests in their ability to abstract the
nature of a thing from the thing itself and hold it sepa-
rately in their minds. Hence they deal in *principles* not
facts.

AVOID FACTS

If you would be a master of conversation, avoid facts.
Specific experience is the subject matter of news report-
ing, but not of conversation. Conversation is a mutual,
intellectual activity having as its purpose the discovery
of new truth, new theory, new angles of knowledge. It
is primarily speculative or argumentative; its operation

illuminates, rather than conveys, any new knowledge.

Practice at speaking in terms of generalities or general principles; avoid specific facts. Turn philosopher, observer, commentator, critic; *and drop your role of news reporter!* Just think—no matter how strange or new the subject—think! You are bound to have some experience on it; reflect on this experience and connect it up with the conversation by means of some general deduction you have made. Let your thinking power, your intelligence, be the fuel for your words!

When you were given the power of speech, it was not intended that you use it to compete with the phonograph. Use it to express your intelligence. Intelligence embodied in spoken words is conversation. Without intelligence, there can be no true conversation.

4. BECOME A PUBLIC SPEAKER

You have no choice whatsoever on this subject! Either you become a capable public speaker or you can never be a real big-shot. All the reputation you have built up for yourself and your special ability can be spoiled in one poor performance on the public rostrum.

And sooner or later you will be confronted with the definite task of making a speech. It will be the occasion that simply cannot be avoided! For, though you pride yourself on skillful maneuvers that helped you escape from making a speech in the past, the time is surely coming when you will have to make that fatal speech.

39

Why dread it so fearfully? Why not face it sanely, yes even enthusiastically, knowing that the opportunity to speak in public offers one of the quickest and surest ways to sell yourself. *Provided, of course, you make a good performance.*

THE FIRST RULE

The first rule for public speaking is PREPARE. The actor rehearses and so does any other prudent individual who exposes his personality to public criticism. If you don't prepare, you will make a miserable performance. One half a minute after you have started, the audience will know that you didn't prepare. They will feel the slight instantly, and out of resentment bear down on discovering your flaws and shortcomings. When you prepare, you compliment your audience; they like to know that you thought them worthy of the necessary work preceding your appearance.

LOUDLY AND CLEARLY

Speak *loudly* and *clearly* enough so that everyone in the room or the hall can hear every word you say. This rule seems unnecessary to mention, yet nine public speakers out of ten neglect to follow it. It is far better to speak too loud than not loud enough; and of course it is impossible to speak too clearly. Most people's hearing apparatus is not up to par; most rooms or halls have air pockets or acoustical handicaps which must be overcome by the speaker. Speak loudly, speak clearly.

ADMIT NO WEAKNESS

Admit or publish *no weakness* concerning yourself. Never apologize for lack of preparation, never confess you have nothing to say, and under no circumstances inform the audience you have a cold, a sore throat, a train to catch, or anything else that is negative. People everywhere take you at your own rating; one word, one syllable of negation will spoil your whole speech and unsell your audience on you.

DO SOMETHING POSITIVE

It's always good to do *something positive* as you start your speech; if this positive act is spontaneous and unpremeditated, it is even better. To change your position on the stage or at the table before starting, to walk a few steps out of your way and move some object or other, stamps you at once as a strong man, a good actor.

AVOID THE MIKE

Most business speakers are poor and incompetent; a little study in the tricks of the trade will make you an outstanding speaker.

It's well to *avoid the microphone* entirely — speakers make a dive for it, glue their faces to it, and automatically lose all expression and individuality. Only a handful of accomplished speakers have been known to use the microphone effectively. The hall or room in which you are speaking was built before radio was invented. The architect made it possible for the human voice — your human voice — to fill every nook and corner of that room unaided, provided you try. Pass up the microphone deliberately — give your speech unassisted and it will be YOUR speech!

GO IN EMPTY

And *go in empty!* Most speakers use notes; a good many read their speech from manuscript. Both methods are absolutely wrong. The second you look down to consult a note, that instant you let your audience relax. And a relaxed audience is no audience at all. You can prepare your talk — if you only apply yourself — so perfectly that neither notes nor manuscript are necessary. This is the ideal speech. Know all you are going to say from memory, say it, and your audience will marvel at your competency.

How would you feel if you went to a play and the actors read their lines from the script, or frequently consulted notes to prompt themselves? That's exactly how your audience feels if you go into your speech visibly reinforced with any material other than your own memory and mind. Go in empty!

HOW YOU SAY IT

Oratory, since time began, has been one of the greatest of the arts. All orators and students of the oratorical art agree that it isn't what you say but *how you say it* that counts most.

As you speak, *act!* Keep your hands out of your pockets; throw them into the air in natural gestures. An easy way to slip into natural gesturing is through *a generous use of the left hand* — it gives an even more graceful accent than the right. Lead with the left and the right will take care of itself.

As you speak, *walk!* Don't stay rooted in one spot. Get your body as well as your voice into action; you break the visual monotony with the motion of your body just as the different inflections of your voice break the oral monotony.

CONCENTRATE

Concentrate! It's better to have one good speech than a hundred miscellaneous ones.

Work on your audience, never allow them to work on you. Always seek to be remembered by some action impulse you planted in them.

Public speaking is an absolute essential in your program of selling yourself. Every great man in business, politics, society, religion, was and is a good public speaker. This job must be attended to — work at it till you've mastered it. The rewards of oratory are even more delectable than those of salesmanship — through self-stimulation and exaltation oratory brings you the highest pleasures known to man! When you work on *them,* they forget to criticize you. You become grand, glorious when you give them something to take away.

43

Writing

1. WRITE!

William Randolph Hearst hit the nail on the head when he announced: "Anyone who can think, can write!" That definitely means that when you confess you are no writer, you admit you cannot think.

And you MUST write to make your expression comprehensive.

In conversation you touch one or a few people.

In public speaking you reach a crowd of hundreds. But in writing you reach millions, and not only in this present moment but in the years to come.

To neglect writing is to forfeit your best chance for universal expression. Before you die, you should have written at least one book, something that exists outside of you, something that will live after you. And the way to get a book to your credit is to *write* it.

How does one write? Samuel Johnson gave the cue beautifully: "Anyone may write, if he will set himself doggedly to it!" That's the way to insure an output. Sit down in front of that typewriter, and in spite of all temptations to delay or renig, start tapping the keys and stick to it! Something will come, and three times out of four it will be worth while enough that, as you read it over to yourself, you will enjoy it immensely!

The big secret in all writing for the non-professional is: loosen up! The very thought of writing something serious may make your blood run cold. You freeze up into a formality that is stiff, uninteresting and miserable. You sweat blood as you write it.

But loosen up and have some fun. Start a sentence and finish it even before you reach the verb. Throw those periods around with reckless abandon. Forget all about unity, coherence and emphasis, and presto, all three show up gloriously!

Write! It's as easy as the willingness to try it and the perseverance to stay with it.

2. WRITE IN VOLUME

You can never be acknowledged a bona fide writer till you have demonstrated your ability to produce in VOLUME.

As you stop in at your book store and see on the shelves those amazing books three inches thick of a thousand pages or more, you wonder how on earth any mortal man could sustain his strength and his ability to pound out all those words. You know very well you could never write a book that big, that long.

But if you have the aspiration to write, you make a big mistake in conceding you are incapable of such a long book.

Volume doesn't insure quality — not by a long shot. But volume is the best known identification of *writing ability*.

Imagine yourself having written a thousand page book, sustaining unity, accuracy, and interest all through the work. Wouldn't you know in your heart—

45

what you very strongly doubt now—that YOU WERE A
WRITER?

So go after volume. Make every word, every phrase,
every sentence, as fine as you can — but for your own
writing morale turn in a VOLUME PERFORMANCE early!
It will make you a writer! For writing, if it is anything,
is *proof of work*. A brilliant poem, a sparkling page
may be proof of *soul* — but thousands of pages and millions of words are uncontradictable proof that you have
strength, wind, heart — the ability to play the game till
the last inning is over. Writing is work and volume tells
whether you're a lazy lout, a butterfly or a he-man of
the craft.

3. TOOT YOUR OWN HORN

Toot your own horn; because if you don't, nobody else
will.

It is necessary that you lay out a definite plan of publicity and promotion in your own behalf. Publicity is
simply the record of your current life written on the
attention and memory of the public. It would be lovely
if you had some friend or attentive assistant who would
do this for you, keeping you constantly in the public
eye, writing and causing to have published many ac-
counts of your brilliant and noble deeds so that the
world at large might know of your genius and valor.
But alas! You can search as long and as far as you want
and never find such a person.

There is only one man competent to act as your publicity agent and that man is *you*.

46

Any time you see a certain name breaking into print, a certain figure appearing in newspapers, magazines, on screen and radio, be sure of this point: that man himself is not only prompting, he is executing, most of his own publicity.

If the big guns feel and acknowledge they have to do it themselves, poor little you shouldn't be ashamed or reluctant to act as your own publicity man.

Don't let modesty interfere with your tactics. Of course, it is repulsive to have to write or engineer some story or event that is extremely favorable to yourself, *but go ahead and do it:* salve your conscience with this philosophy: it's got to be done and no one else will do it if you don't!

I know of no rule for advancing yourself by means of publicity better than this one:

Let not a single day pass without engineering at least one FORMAL *piece of publicity in your own behalf!*

By formal, I mean, you definitely take aim at a certain mark and shoot at it. To hit will be favorable, to miss will do no harm. At least one attempt every day! What a program! What a consistent, provident, rational action for any man who cares about selling himself!

Working publicity is simply working the law of averages: you write a letter, an article, you contrive to have yourself placed on a certain committee, to get your name in print, to make a speech, to be seen, heard and recognized by the public in a public place. If the attempt fails in its full objective, it will certainly succeed in this small sphere: the person at whom you have aimed it in hopes of its being publicized, even while he turns you down, will appraise you as an alert, aggressive and deserving individual and though he refuses you this time will most likely grant your request next time.

In publicity, the guiding rule is: *Don't be modest!* If you let your modesty get the best of you, you will lose countless opportunities for publicizing yourself.

Acting

1. PUT ON A FRONT AND GET AWAY WITH IT!

They always judge the book by its cover. There's nothing can take the place of *front*. A good personal appearance will get any man by, with scarcely any aid from any other quality, but all other qualities put together have a hard job getting any man by, if he doesn't make a good personal appearance.

Some of the things that make a bad appearance:

> Cheap Clothes
> Poor Posture
> Too Fat
> Too Skinny
> Bad Complexion
> Bad Teeth
> Need a Haircut
> Dirty

48

GAMBLE ON GOOD CLOTHES

There's no mistake as bad as paying too little money for your clothes.

When you buy a suit, the price tag is always removed before you wear it. But the price is still visible to everybody you meet. Whether he's observing or not, everyone notices your clothes unconsciously and knows just about how much they cost.

Here's the best test for your clothes:

How many suits have you today of which you would be ashamed to own up to the price?

If you're ashamed of the low price you paid, don't think the matter is private information with you. The supposed secret is obvious to everyone who ever saw the suit on you.

Wear a suit that cost a sum of money that you considered quite daring to pay. Every time you put this suit on, you feel quite daring all over again. This is a great way to feel especially when all people recognize that you have a foundation for your daring. Though most men theoretically recognize the value of expensive clothes, few are good sports enough to go all the way and lay their money on the line. So when you boldly place a bet on yourself and pay the extra premium, you instantly enter a select group.

A good suit of clothes is the key to the highest personal morale. Be a good gambler and buy this morale with hard earned money—people judge a book by its cover, and every good book ought to have a good cover!

49

POSTURE MAKES "THAT HANDSOME MALE"

Of all the elements that go to make front, perhaps none is as important as posture.

Many rules for selling yourself to others involve two sides, you and the others. To get people to like you, for instance, requires both your doing something and their doing something.

But a thing like posture deals with only one side—yours. The control is entirely in your hands and there is no chance of failure if you exercise this control. You don't have to rest your success on the vagaries of human nature (other than your own)!

To command a good posture you simply command yourself. You stand up straight, if you are standing. You sit up straight if you are sitting. You throw your shoulders back and pull your stomach in. You just don't do these things once a day—you do them all day long. No special exercises are necessary other than a positive command from you to you, an order easy to understand and easy to execute.

You stand up straight when you are getting measured for a suit—because you feel the tailor is observing you closely and you want to make a good impression on him. You then realize that posture is a very good means of making an impression.

Men—when you shift your eyes or turn your heads to look at a girl walking down the street—hasn't she always a good *posture?*

Ladies—when you find your glances being attracted

toward that handsome male just passing by—hasn't he always a good *posture?*

And when either of you sees an individual with stooped shoulders, drooping, shapeless body—a poor posture—don't you quit looking quickly?

Posture is simply a command from you to you. It's all in your hands. It has two very fine results. It gives you a great deal more pep for doing oceans of work, and it improves your looks to the point where you definitely make a big impression on others. It also makes you "appearance-conscious" thereby toning up all the departments that concern appearance.

There are two simple ways to develop posture:

THINK OF SOMEONE WHO'S VERY STRAIGHT

There's a person you know who stands very straight, walks very straight, carries himself or herself very straight. Head aloft, chest out, stomach in, what a fine figure!

Think of that person—there's a picture of him and her already in your mind, simply because a remarkable carriage makes such a great impression on you—and so it's easy to recall the image of the young, graceful, inspiring body.

Think of that person who's very straight. You find yourself lifting your head, pulling your stomach in, throwing your chest out.

Perhaps you can't be as young as he or she is—but you can be as straight. Keep the image before you.

THINK OF SOMEONE WHO'S VERY STOOPED

Think of someone with drooping body, bent shoulders, an old man before his time.

The very thought straightens you up instantly for you hate to think that a similar fate should be yours.

That stooped over person is a fine example of what lack of posture will do to you. It will rob you of energy, turn you into an old man, and make you unsightly in the eyes of the world. Change yourself while there's time!

COME "CLEAN"!

From the standpoint of impression, your body is like a plate of food served to a patron in a restaurant.

If the food is dirty, greasy, sloppy; the dish chipped, the silverware tarnished and bent, the patron is not going to relish the meal. Neither is anyone going to relish you, if your body is dirty, greasy, or untidy. You've heard the expression, "I simply can't stomach him!" People actually do accept or reject another's personality on the strength of appearance.

Keep clean. A daily bath should be a reality not just a happy contemplation. Daily change of underwear and linen is also essential to that "clean feeling." And if you feel clean to yourself, you always look clean to others. A clean body creates a chemical attraction which is the first step in winning a personal following. Of course, it is not as potent as personality, but personality has to be mighty powerful if it is lacking!

2. SHOW SOME SPIRIT!

Spirit is what you put into it.

In a little more highfalutin' language, spirit is the intensifying, the concentration, of all your life force into one single act.

You are alive. You just don't prove your life to the world by going through the functions that every vegetable, whether plant, animal or human expresses. The fact that your hair grows, that your finger nails grow is merely chemical proof that you are a vegetable.

But how do you prove that you're an exponent of real human life, that you belong to the rational order! By spirit!

Your life is *yours* and your life force should be instantly at your command. If it is, you can generate spirit in an instant, can deliver this magic quality in any and all places, and move everyone within your sight or hearing to notice you, to fear you, to respect you, to love you, to follow you, to copy you, to do whatever your spirit dictates.

Think of three people you know well who have gotten anywhere. Haven't all three an overabundance of spirit? In fact, do you know anyone who ever made any progress in the world of human beings who didn't have spirit?

To develop spirit should be your first aim, if you haven't it already. If you have it, SHOW IT! Show it at every opportunity. But if you haven't it, here are a few ways to get it!

CONCENTRATE WITH ZIP AND EMPHASIS!

Concentrate on the fact that you're alive! Think of yourself as a living, powerful, individual person with feelings, thoughts, impulses and aspirations. Just contemplate this life force inside you. As you look at it, think about it, you *feel* it much more definitely, and as soon as you feel it, you are ready to express it.

Concentrate your *life force!* Don't live in the whole wide world, live definitely in the confines of your own body. Don't dilute your life, pull life toward you. *Concentrate!*

As soon as you train yourself to concentrate on your life force, just that soon are you bringing your spirit under definite control. Concentration produces both the presence of spirit and the control of that spirit.

Anger is spirit. You can't imagine someone angry and distracted at the same time. No! The angry man is concentrating.

Concentrate your *life* in the *act!* Just go out to perform any task with spirit. Chop some wood, walk a mile, make a sales talk, all the while *concentrating on your own powers of life.* The task is done with immense speed, with zip and emphasis, with elation and vibration, qualities which you generate as you go along.

PERSONALITY—CHILD OF SPIRIT

Many people will tell you that the man who best knows how to sell himself is the man who has personality.

54

Personality is simply one department of spirit. If you have spirit, you automatically have personality.

Just develop the power to concentrate your life force on *anything* and you'll find you're advancing your own ideas, you're expressing your own peculiar characteristics, you're playing on the emotions of others, with *spirit*. The sum of such activities is *personality*.

CULTIVATE THAT RADICAL STREAK

It's pretty hard to be a man of spirit, unless you also have a slightly radical streak. This does not mean you should be a bolshevik or an anarchist.

You are radical when your convictions are really convictions. When your convictions so move you, that you simply cannot bear to see the opposite conditions maintain.

All lovers of truth are radicals, for great things like truth, liberty and justice are the most exciting elements in the world when they have been damaged, attacked, or perverted. No man can bear to see them disparaged or abrogated without going radical!

If you have a slightly radical streak, don't seek to squelch it. Be proud of the fact that you feel strongly on some particular subject, strongly enough to fight for what you consider right, to contradict the world when it seeks to disrupt or besmirch this truth. To defend your side of the case, you are bound to call on your store of spirit, and that's really all it takes to get spirit, is to *call on yourself for some.*

55

Spirit is what you put into it. What you have to put into it is your own life force. Concentrate! Intensify! Compress a hundred years into a second—and you have spirit—and along with it the power to move any man or group of men your way.

3. BE AN EGOTIST—AND MAKE THEM LIKE IT!

You can't get yourself across in the form of a cloud, a dream, or a gentle rainfall of pleasant little characteristics.

You have to go across in one fell swoop as a definite, exact, forceful EGO—you have to be an egotist, if you're going to get across at all!

Men say of a successful fellow man, "He sure thinks a lot of himself!" "He has the big head!" "Who does he think he is anyway?"

Why, the man thinks he's SOMEBODY—and the remarkable thing about it is HE IS SOMEBODY!

Be an egotist. Don't distribute your personality all over creation—wrap it into one hard, clear, NAMED character—yourself! Write your name all over the page, sign everything you do, be sure you and you alone are getting YOUR OWN life force across to the others.

Don't use the WORD "I," but use the thought "I" and the meaning "I" continuously—be sure your I, your EGO, is writing itself all over the face of the globe every minute of the day. Only in egotism can you achieve individuality. Only in egotism can you get others to notice you, remember you, advertise you. Be an egotist!

THAT SMALL IDEA YOU HAVE OF YOURSELF

Now be honest. You often reflect to yourself over your own personality. View yourself as in a mirror, appraise your thoughts, your weaknesses, your abilities. And you generally come out of the huddle with a pretty small and cheap idea of yourself!

Don't be alarmed. The same thing happens to everybody else.

You see an upstanding man, a man supposedly in a higher stratum of society or higher up the ladder of business than you, and you just can't imagine yourself being in his class. The man is big. He does things in a big way. He has big thoughts, big ability, he's used to the best!

But if you were allowed to pry inside that very man's heart you would find, that instead of being used to the best, he's common, cheap, and just as little as you. He leaves a ring around the washstand after he washes his face and hands. He has blackheads, trouble with his laundry, grumbles about his meals at home, and would probably be knocked unconscious were he to discover himself coming down with just one original idea. He knows many men in a much higher stratum than his and he has despaired of ever reaching *their level!*

The first thing for you to realize is that this small idea you have of yourself is *universal.* Everybody else has a small idea of himself. Everybody else, in his own introspection, can see nothing but commonness, plainness, cheapness.

57

Now knowing the condition, can't you see what an opportunity lies in your changing YOUR attitude?

Though you have a small idea of yourself now, you don't have to keep it! And just because other men have the same small ideas of themselves, you don't have to be like them. Rise above them! Be fine! Think fine things! Develop the fine attitude! *Class* starts by *regarding yourself as possessing it*. As soon as you get that classy idea and abandon the small idea, you instantly become what the world considers a BIG man.

Get rid of that small idea of yourself. Give them what they want. BE BIG!

4. ENTHUSIASM—THE QUALITY THAT NEVER FAILS

When you're full of enthusiasm, you're full of magic. It's the one human quality that never fails.

The Greeks who invented the word saw the miracle of it, for enthusiasm means "God in us!" Enthusiasm is a quality at once animal and divine, and that's why it can't fail. People see the emotion of common feeling joined with the ecstasy of spirit and must respond.

Warm up! Believe in yourself! Get excited! Feel the full spiritual force of your case, of your aspirations— let the world see your pride, your faith, the fire in your blood, the full heavenly courage of your convictions. Enthuse and the world enthuses with you. Enthuse and the power of the gods is yours! Don't save your enthusiasm for a "special occasion" when you think it will be most effective. Use it ALL the time!

TURN IT ON!

Do you want enthusiasm? Well, turn it on! The easiest and quickest way to get enthusiastic is to *decide* to be enthusiastic. First, you may have to kid yourself. Your sane, normal self may see no reason for your getting "hot and bothered." But go ahead and deliberately—artificially—turn on the enthusiasm, saying to yourself, "This thing is great!" "I'm wild about it!" "Nothing can stop me!"

Throw yourself into a trance and leave this commonplace, ordinary world for the man-made heaven of enthusiasm. Seek it. Demand it. Order it. Don't let yourself be distracted, cooled off, or confused. You are going to get enthusiastic. Turn on the enthusiasm!

LISTEN TO THE SOUND OF YOUR OWN VOICE

When another speaks, you listen to his words, to the sound of his voice, When *you* speak, the other person hears your voice, *but you don't!* In the act of thinking of what you are saying, and observing how your words are taking with your listener, you fail to hear your own voice.

It's important that YOU DO HEAR yourself. The enthusiastic person ALWAYS hears his own voice. Its strange, familiar, personal quality stirs him, causes him to vibrate more highly, produces a resonance that is a magical self-stimulant.

Speak now and listen to yourself talking. It sounds

59

funny, your voice is your own, you know, but it seems like it has no right to be speaking at all. But in a second, you reflect, it has every right, your words are YOU, and your thoughts are worthy thoughts. As you listen, you strain to make your voice "good." You put on extra steam, you speak a little louder. A richness of inflection enters, a depth of vibration, you have your audience rocking and yourself stimulated past all previous heights of enthusiasm. Just listen to your own voice!

SEE THAT YOU YOURSELF ARE SOLD

You can hardly be an enthusiastic person, unless you're sold on yourself. You can hardly deliver enthusiasm to a cause, unless you're sold on the cause.

First of all believe in yourself. Cease thinking about your deficiencies, your weakness, your lack of ability. Contemplate your good points, dwell on your prowess. You're pretty good. You know you're pretty good!

You'll find it hard to generate enthusiasm, unless you sincerely know and feel you're PRETTY GOOD. Once you establish this self-respect, once you force yourself to believe you've got something on the ball, enthusiasm immediately appears.

The same principle applies to your cause, your proposition, your product. You can't be enthusiastic about a thing and critical of it at one and the same time. You have to be sold on it. Appraise the good points of your cause, steep yourself in the attractions, the excellences, and think of nothing negative or detracting.

60

BOOST

Throw away your hammer and get a horn! BOOST! Be for the good side! Pull for the success of the project, give it your complete moral backing.

It costs you nothing to be a booster, it's all in your attitude of mind. You think, feel and act positively. You are on the plus end always. By process of praise, encouragement, cheer, support, you *suggest* your side into the winning column. Defeat, disappointment are impossible to a booster.

ASSOCIATE WITH ENTHUSIASTIC PEOPLE

Enthusiasm is a fever, a fever more contagious than any known to medicine. One second after the fever breaks out in you, it breaks out in all people within the range of your voice and personality.

No one can immunize himself to this fever. If a contact is made, the enthusiasm must spread instantly.

So it is very much to your advantage to put your body in those places where enthusiastic people hang out. Meet them, get to know them personally. Engage them in conversation at every possible opportunity. Cultivate them, hold on them; their company is priceless!

You can go anywhere and find morbid, negative, listless, dull people. Bright, stimulating, enthusiastic people are hard to find. But sooner or later you meet them —and *remember* them.

Write down a list of all the people you know who

61

are enthusiastic. It won't be very long. Let them be your first sources of enthusiasm and make it your business to see and talk to them as much as possible. No such meeting can ever fail to develop enthusiasm in you.

HAVE A GOAL—REACH IT!

The college football team gets enthusiastic because it has a goal. It wants to win and it knows exactly what constitutes the winning.

Have a definite goal, a destiny for all your hopes, ambitions, and energies. Decide to reach that goal no matter what gets in your way. If you really want it you will have it and day by day you will make definite progress toward it. As you continuously contemplate the goal and note the progress you are making toward it, you will become more and more enthusiastic. Always know where you're going; never vary from your course; this determination will never let your enthusiasm wane.

SLICE OFF A PIECE OF THE FUTURE

Enthusiasm minimizes what has gone, glorifies what is to come. It brings the future into the present and allows you to enjoy things that are coming.

FROM THE INSIDE OUT!

Where does it come from? From the inside out! Enthusiasm is immanent action, life action. The proud peacock, the cackling hen, the singing lark take what they have inside them and throw it out to the world. So with your enthusiasm. It can't be sliced like sausage, handled like a brick, or sold like stock and bonds. It is action entirely from within—*your* action.

Look for it inside yourself—just make it visible unto yourself and soon it will be visible to the entire world!

IGNORE THE HANDICAPS

Enthusiasm ignores all handicaps, disregards past failures, refuses to acknowledge any restrictions. Even the practical and the mechanical are often forgotten by the enthusiast and in the fever of his enthusiasm it is proved that enthusiasm is *even more practical* than the practical and the mechanical. For the sublime, inspired man, glorying in the sweetness of his objective, has no time for the practical "handicaps" and can't entertain them against a possible lowering of his own enthusiasm.

Most of the things that have been declared "impossible" were truly impossible—without enthusiasm. By practical mechanical law they couldn't be done. But by the divine sweep of enthusiasm new law was introduced —and they were done.

Ignore the handicaps! To dwell on the handicaps is only to weaken your own cause. To appraise the opposition fairly is to give the opposition assistance. Enthusiasm is prejudiced, narrow, one-sided—it sees only its own end—allows no resistance or negative thing to enter. It has no time for adversity. It recognizes no

63

adversary and never fights, never argues, simply because it is totally blind to all opposition.

FASTER! FASTER!

Speed up! You have not a minute to waste. If you're enthusiastic you demand a quick conclusion, you simply haven't the time to let nature take its course. Hurry on to your goal, stopping for nothing, deferring to nothing, racing, racing, all the time. Speed up. Dive into your subject and BEGIN THE THING. With a mighty swath you can do a life's work in an hour! For TIME even, most ruthless of all the elements, succumbs to enthusiasm!

Speed up! Work quickly, immediately, frantically. Take no time to breathe, to cool off, to rest. Your own enthusiasm is the only energy you need. Time and space must be given no standing whatsoever! Do it, do it now. Hurry! Hurry! Hurry! No man can loaf and be enthusiastic.

BE A CHILD AGAIN

Enthusiasm? It's the quality a kid has as Christmas approaches!

The kid believes in Christmas—he's for it a hundred per cent. When he goes downtown to look at the toys, when he sees Santa Claus, there's nothing listless, indifferent or *blah* in the kid's deportment. He's excited! He's interested! He's alive! He's ENTHUSIASTIC.

It's not the kid but the kid's *enthusiasm* that makes

Christmas the greatest time of all. Enthusiasm is almighty, irresistible, unfailing. It's the most contagious of all fevers. When the kid becomes infected with it, everybody in his immediate vicinity catches it, too. His *cause* goes over because no cause actuated by real enthusiasm can ever fail!

If you want to glow with real enthusiasm, be a real child again. Light up with the intense possession, in your spirit, of the object you are seeking. Jump about, rave, talk it up—like a kid talks up Christmas. Let yourself go ALL THE WAY. The kid is entirely off guard —the bars are down. He not only doesn't care what the world thinks of him, he doesn't even know it is thinking.

Be consumed with your subject to the point of childishness. Perhaps the sublime miracle of all enthusiasts is that they are children. So never try to hide your simplicity, eagerness, emotional regard for your objective.

Creating

1. INVENT THINGS, INVENT IDEAS

There are two main kinds of invention; the invention of things and the invention of ideas. Invent! It is a most worthy form of expression. It is an everlasting testimonial to your personality.

Edison invented the electric light and ever after the electric light became an expression of Edison and his genius. The invention lives on—a permanent advertisement of the inventor.

The easiest avenue to invention is *consideration*. Put yourself in the user's place. Go with your mind into his body and see what you can do to make things more convenient, more comfortable, more enjoyable and more practical for him.

For sixteen years engineers worked on motor cars, perfecting engine, chassis and body. Suddenly one day one of them happened to remember that an automobile is always used outdoors, that often while outdoors it starts to rain, that rain falling on the windshield made driving extremely difficult and hazardous, and so he thought of an automatic windshield wiper!

Every good invention is an OBVIOUS thing. As soon as you see it for the first time, you say, "Why didn't I think of it before?" The reason you didn't think of it was because you failed to show consideration. You failed to go with your mind into a different place than where your own body was at the time you were thinking. To be an inventor this is the main ability you must cultivate; to see the thing from the other's point of view.

The only other process in invention is to blindly try something, anything. All such attempts at invention suddenly wind up with the ambitious inventor going straight back to the thing on which he is trying to improve and seeking to change it.

By far the better road, whether you are seeking to invent things or ideas, is to throw everything that has already been done overboard and start from scratch. This way you say that nothing is necessary and nothing is impossible. You are not fettered by old burdens, old ways, and very often something entirely new, refreshing and useful presents itself.

Especially in the field of ideas. Abandon the old stuff and take a shot at something new. Make an assumption that is the direct contradiction of the thing everyone accepts as true, and see what interesting new theories and ideas you unearth. Deliberately set about proving this radical new thing and immediately you have a whole world of fresh idea material to draw from.

A somewhat less substantial way of developing new ideas is to follow the child's plan. The child boldly soars into the realm of dreams and fantasy and brings down some interesting and distracting things, but not very often any solid ideas.

Ideas and things are best invented by throwing the past overboard. Apply yourself religiously to the business of invention. One of the biggest rewards of invention is the thrill that you have reproduced yourself out of yourself. You have certified your own right to existence by proving that you can cause still more existence. And, furthermore, if you are a good inventor, you will be the best kind of a self-advertiser, and arrange, through your invention, for the world to hear constantly and insistently that you are a man in a million.

2. STEAL FROM THE CLOCK—AND PRODUCE

The most active, solid, and definite form of expression is production.

You make a thing. The thing is physical, visible,

touchable by others. It is truly a part of you, a reproduction of you. You can go away from it, and it will remain there as a testimonial of you, of your quality, your ability, your spirit. And it will not just be a transient, evanescent expression of you—*it will last!*

Produce! There is no substitute for production. There is no thrill, no satisfaction like you will find in production. It is a man's game and it involves a man's duty and a man's pride. Produce!

Any effort to produce involves two things—*you* and *hours.*

Production takes energy—you furnish that. You have more than enough energy, if you only will to use it in actual production. To feel weak or tired is simply to admit you have no desire, no instinct for production. *You want to loaf.*

It's pretty hard to express yourself by going to dances and ball games, by wasting hours in idle gossip and useless rag chewing, listening to the radio, reading light "pastime" books, sleeping, vacationing, playing jokes or tricks on other people. All these are devices to avoid production.

But if you have the energy and the will, production is easy! "Provided," you will say, "you *have the time!*"

You have the time—there is always plenty of time to produce! No matter how much of your time is taken up in detailed or routine jobs or the mechanical needs of living, there is always a big margin left out of every day in which you can do some real and independent production.

68

Produce! The real producers are the same kind of people as you; they lose the same average number of hours you do every day in necessary work that can hardly be called production, but can't be avoided; they have the same temptations to rest, and loaf, and escape *extra burdens* on their energy, yet they drive themselves to steal from the rest of their day, REALLY THE ONLY PART OF THE DAY THAT BELONGS TO THEM, the time in which to produce.

The real producers are the people who grab at the extra hours and use them for personal production. And almost the only distinction between these people and the average run of fellow mortals is that *they have used their extra time!*

Produce! All the sources and materials of production are right inside you. Seize those soft dreamy hours that are now sifting so noiselessly through your fingers and use them for production!

GO ON A "WORK BENDER"

Excesses of all kinds are dangerous but, there's no getting away from it, you will indulge in excess every once in a while.

If you have the excess complex pretty heavy, see if you can't throw some of these excesses into the legitimate column.

For instance, work. Every once in a while go on a "work bender." Work right through a whole night without going to bed. Work fanatically and exaggeratedly every second of a given day, not allowing yourself the slightest distraction or diversion.

You often excused some of your excesses by saying, "I can only go so long, and then I have to blow off steam." Well, try blowing off some of that steam in the legitimate channels of abnormal work. There will be a hangover, of course; but the hangover will be charged with pride of accomplishment instead of brutal remorse, and your constitution will not have been hurt in the least!

☆

SECTION 2

Promise

The rational man is interested in the past. And on occasion he can bring himself to live in the past, for well he knows that the laws of human nature, cause and effect, never change. Out of an analysis of the past he can gain access to the future. But the rational man is too rare a species for you to bother with. Though the past appeals to *him, you* needn't pay too much attention to it.

But the *present?* From childhood, we have been led to believe that there is only one kind of time—the present. That our only chance to do anything is the here and now. This teaching is, of a certainty, true, but you must remember that when you are selling yourself you do not necessarily use what is true but rather what is *expedient.*

Now, actually, there is only one type of person who

possesses the ability to live in the present—in fact who is ABLE TO LIVE AT ALL. That is the *high-keyed* individual whose mind and sensitory system are composed of a million springs; whose intensity, resiliency, vibrancy are beyond definition, limitless in scope. This type of man wants only the present, understands only the present, has no time for the past or the future, because he wants to live *now*. His type of life may not be as high in quality as the rational life but it is much more intense.

But you don't need to worry much about catering to the high-keyed man—for alas! He is even more rare than the rational man, and even if you did find him, you would soon discover that he would be working on you instead of your working on him!

This brings us to the third type of individual, that class of people who live life only potentially, being neither truly rational nor high-keyed. The only time that exists for them is the *future*.

Their closest approach to any kind of living is the dream, or the *imagined life*. They care nothing about the past, ignore the present entirely, and spend all of their conscious hours in contemplating the future and its wonders. The mainspring of their life is hope; and if you would hold them in the palm of your hand, it is up to you to kindle this hope and keep it perpetually alive.

1. TALK OF TOMORROW

Your promise is simply the size of your future.

Never use the past tense. Never point to the past.

People have forgotten what happened then. To point it out now is merely to tell them they are too unintelligent to have a memory. And because they have no memory, they still don't believe that what you say happened actually did happen.

Never use the present tense. To say that something is actually so NOW is to demand either an admission or a denial. But people are in no position to give either. For they are so lacking in observation and critical ability that most of them are blind to the present and the rest of them unable to digest it. To throw it in their faces is insulting and angering.

But—the future! Ah, the future! There is something EVERYBODY understands, the only world they will ever know. It is always there!

As long as the future is so delightful, why not let it always be pleasant and promising? Why paint black skies, foreboding clouds and stormy seas? That is promise of destruction, not promise of life! The rosy future is the only future; if you present any other, you will drive people away from you.

You are always safe in offering them a grand future —provided you permanently remain in the future tense. What if the future you spoke of yesterday is here now —don't commit the folly of speaking of it, for it is now the present and no experienced campaigner deigns to mention the present. Talk of tomorrow.

Your handling of the future and of your own personal promise must always link you with those you are selling. Your promise is their promise; if you make

73

good, they make good. That good must always be a community good. It must reflect their sagacity in predicting your success. And it must always involve your recognition of their support, the sharing of your success with them.

Tie your promise to your people.

2. PASS THE WHITE MEAT

The future is a great uncharted territory—everybody's home, everybody's haven. It's uncharted for them—*so you be the one who charts it!*

Your chart will be what is known as a Plan or a Program, the "white meat" of life's roast.

A plan is merely a catalog of contemplated operations, and the expected outcome of said operations—all of which are to happen in the future. It's a public, open, visual demonstration of the objective and of the necessary means for achieving that objective.

So when you are building a plan for someone else's benefit, be sure that its objective coincides perfectly with his wishes, and that the means you suggest for accomplishing the end are the activities with which he is in sympathy.

This is indeed the perfect plan—the thing no normal man can resist.

A plan is practical if, after it receives the necessary O. K., its machinery can begin moving at once. No one expects the end to be achieved quickly, in fact we are often led to believe that those who have the power to

74

endorse the plan are best satisfied *if the end is never
achieved.* But it is highly important that the machinery
be ready to start immediately. This action completes the
miracle of bringing the future directly into the present,
one of life's greatest thrills.

Have a plan! The man capable of devising a plan,
of comprehensively developing a sane and logical program of betterment, gains the respect of the entire
world. Planners are really rare—but they shouldn't be,
for a plan is really easy to do! In framing any plan, be
sure to observe these three basic rules:

1. Cite your objective.

2. Cite your means, naming the order in which
   they will be undertaken from the present on.

3. Justify your plan by weighing costs against
   benefits, and illuminate the practicality of its
   operations.

If you have a plan, no one can say of you: "What's
he after? What's he want? He doesn't know what it's
all about."

Aim at something. Decide on the definite means of
achievement. Formalize the end and the means in a
concrete shape and you have a plan. It's a great way
to offer up to a hungry populace a delicious slice of the
future, for the future is what they revel in, and what,
incidentally, they never have.

8. DON'T LET THEM PIN A LABEL ON YOU

Let people become suspicious of your many gifts and abilities, but never let them know *all* you can do.

As soon as they are able to label you, they will; and after that *you will have no more promise.*

One way to keep your abilities unknown is *never allow yourself to be put to a public test.* By good publicity, and propaganda you may have acquired the reputation of being very artistic. If you know you aren't artistic, but still find the reputation useful, it would be folly to lose that reputation by attempting an art performance, such as drawing a picture, or making a design, in front of the people who idolize you. Your sorry performance would destroy your valuable reputation, and your artistic promise would instantly disappear as soon as you became known.

Give off indications of abilities, but carefully avoid the public test. In few subjects, indeed, can any man of promise fulfill his promise. His deeds either have to be sensational, or normal; if normal (as most deeds are) the promise is lost, and no man can keep on producing a string of sensational deeds.

Once you have shown everything you have done, you have revealed everything you CAN do. There ends your promise. The artist or writer who trots in every sample of work he ever did destroys his own promise—for the very size of the volume announces that he may not have much more of the stuff left in him.

People judge you not by your best but by your worst

76

work. Never display anything inferior that you have done; bury it.

Never display all the good things you have done, for in them you are offering the world a measure of yourself. The measured man is the man whose promise is past. Just show a few samples—THE FEWER THE BETTER! But make those few good. Then the person who is thinking of hiring you, promoting you, voting for you, will, in his mind's eye, dream about the multitude of other good things you will do in the future, things that seem far better in his imagination than you could ever make them look in reality.

Hold something back and you will arouse people's curiosity—they will watch you, pay attention to you, look forward to your future deeds. "The amateur tries to do it all at once; the pro leaves something for the next time!"

Surround your projects with a touch of mystery. Mystery is created by revealing the part, not the whole; by clever silence; by delicious vagueness and suspense. "I can't say exactly what it is, but it is something good!" "There are a lot of things in the air right now which will bear luscious fruit very shortly!" "I have something sweet I want to show you!" A thousand such tasty morsels can be delivered if you are only careful to put the necessary tincture of mystery into everything you do.

Hint, indicate, suggest your promise. Let the other write in claims for you that you dare not make for yourself. Don't deny or dispel these claims—and never be so foolish as to furnish the material that will destroy your reputation for some special talent. That reputation can be saved forever by keeping the full extent of your possession of that talent unknown.

Little men are not content to dream, to imagine, they have to fix you in their small focus; they have to pin a label on you. They would have you become known as a small specialist, as the fellow who can write good limericks, as the carpenter who does fine work but is awfully slow, as the pitcher with a good curve but no control.

The way to prevent them from pinning any label on you is to anticipate them, and just as the label and pin are poised for the ceremony, by an heroic effort perform some feat directly opposite to what the label encompasses. Don't ever let the little men label you and you will never become little.

4. WHY PEOPLE MARRY

Do you know why people marry?

It is natural, normal, and it's based on biological impulse. That's right. But do you know why people marry *particular* people?

If you're married, you married that girl or fellow because of his or her *promise*. If you're not married, promise is what will decide who your particular mate will be.

Not necessarily promise of worldly advancement, but *promise of happiness*. Promise is the whole basis of all romance. Promise is the activating cause not only of marriage proposals but of all business proposals, all buying and selling.

Promise is the quality that makes up all our dreams —the only place where true happiness can be found.

If you will look back into your personal history, just before you married the girl, if you can remember all your poetic dreams, your idealistic imaginings, your purity of motive, your hopes, your fancies, your fine resolutions, you have a good idea of *exactly the kind of response* the quality of promise can arouse in people today, even when it concerns only matters of general business or practical life.

They call a fine machine a "sweetheart." They say a promising player is a "honey." Thrilling to the things *they are going to do!*

In selling yourself, in achieving public success in a social or business way, this is exactly the figure you must cut for yourself. You are the fiancee of your public; it must thrill to you, love you, be ready to sacrifice all to back you up. The formula for achieving this happy relationship isn't difficult either: just go back to your courtship days and act the same way now toward your public as you did toward your loved one.

If you weren't handsome in face or figure, and still the girl thought you strong, you were strong to her simply because you were *going* to be strong. You told her so. Do the same thing with your public!

If you didn't have any money, you told her how much you were going to make, and because she loved you—

and also because she loved the idea of "going to make it" —she waited. Tell that to your business associates, too, they all know that to make big money they have to wait a while. Ask them to wait a while for you to deliver it— they are reasonable that way!

When you were courting you were faithful, you were attentive, you were sincere! Be that way now—if you would build your new promise now. You were optimistic, hopeful instead of regretful, enthusiastic instead of morose—be that way again. Your public is your sweetheart and you in turn are its sweetheart, and to sell yourself through the quality of promise, you have to relive your courtship days all over again.

5. HAND OUT THE "DREAM STUFF"

To generate promise, you must have the ability to create illusion. You must be able to hand out the stuff out of which dreams are made.

For instance, suppose you are a struggling chemist in a huge laboratory. Just one of a score of men, whose labor is almost standardized, whose future is drab and uninviting.

You want to get somewhere in your work, but you can't by just working. You have to create an illusion.

You go to the top boss and conjure up your illusion. In the back of your mind you have the possible answer to a great chemical problem, something that will revolutionize industry and commerce. You tell him that you want five years to work exclusively on your idea. It cannot be done in shorter time. Although (by accident) it might come about after a month. Neither do you guarantee that even in five years you will come up with the great discovery, but you humbly suggest that the potential reward is worth the effort.

Now, even though the boss turns you down, you have created an illusion. The illusion is that it MAY be possible for you to discover the great secret. Even as you go back to your old job, you have become a new man in the boss's eyes, a worker rich in potentiality and deserving of the first promotion that may occur.

6. "NO IMAGINATION?" HOW SAD!

Vision is the power to see great things—and to see them far ahead.

To open up your eyes and see what is happening *now* —that is merely observation, not vision. But to be able to see things *before* they happen, ah, that is amazing, preternatural, sublime!

If you would have promise you must surely have VISION. The word suggests *seeing,* so you must set about developing your *seeing faculty.* Now the faculty that pries into the future, the inner eye of the mind, is imagination.

How sad it is, when you hear it said of another man: "He has no imagination!" Isn't it exactly the same as saying: "He has no more promise!" Imagination is the faculty that deals with things that don't exist but which may exist in the future. Of course it gets its material from the past and from the present, but that material then is fashioned and reshaped into things more glorious, more beautiful, more valuable than anything ever known in history.

An active imagination is simply the ability to reform things, objects, principles and ideas and bring them out as *new* things never seen before.

To develop imagination, if you haven't it now, you must first develop the ability to reform things in your mind. To change the old into the new. To reshape, repaint; to expand, to join; send the practical thing through the realm of dream so that it comes out still practical, apparently, and yet now is endowed with a dreamy glamour that makes it far more alluring.

The mind—and the imagination is part of the mind —acts either mechanically, which is almost the same as saying automatically, or it acts on individual command from the person owning it, that is to say, individually and creatively. Just the normal happenings of everyday life will give your mind enough mechanical exercise. Practice at making it *create*. Practice at throwing your own individuality into the realm of the mental unseen and unknown, and find out what you can discover from such a journey. When your mind creates, it always comes up with something *new*. That new thing is the direct product of your imagination.

Now just as the mind can creatively *make* things, so also can it creatively *see* things. What it thus sees are visions—grand and glorious vistas of good and unusual things to come.

The world loves vision because it is synonymous with promise. Because it is concerned strictly with the future. Because the future is the most important thing of all!

To have vision is important but even more important is *to let all people know you have it.* So be constantly prophesying and predicting. The great changes, and accomplishments you endorse will surely come, if not in ten years, then surely in twenty-five! This impossible invention will surely come about! This marvelous expansion, this world-wide growth, this far-flung development is the product of your ability to read the future.

If the future is your own private property, and if you make no bones about dictating what it shall look like, what clothes it shall wear and what wonders it shall evolve, then truly you are a man of vision, a child of destiny, and a whole carload of promise!

7. STAY YOUNG THE REST OF YOUR LIFE

An old man can't have promise; promise is the peculiar possession of youth. Stay young!

Even though the years pile up on your body, they needn't molest your mind in any way—in fact, through proper cultivation, you can grow younger as you grow older.

As you graduate from the sophomore stage of your life, you acquire a practical perspective on men, things, and the world of business; you pick up new philosophy which gives you better control of yourself; you develop your personal faculties through practice and experience, and you lose a great deal of the timidity of your youth.

It's a pity that most men—just about this time in their careers—let their physical age so dominate their personality that they give in to a slight touch of baldness or grey hair and consciously become engulfed in that dangerous passage of middle age, which is the first stage of decay.

But leaders don't do that! Leaders stay young! Here's a man in politics who is claiming the attention of the whole world—he is not a young man physically, but he certainly is a young man psychologically. He may be forty, fifty, even sixty years old and yet he is younger than seventy-five per cent of the men who have just passed twenty-five!

A leader never grows old. A GOOD MAN never grows old. Be good enough to stay young!

Stay young! Youth is tireless, energetic; the best way to produce energy is to use what you have.

Stay young! Youth is ever fresh, ever new. Surprise 'em with a new side, a new personality, a new outlook, every time they see you.

Stay young! Youth is daring! Take a chance! Don't reckon the consequences too closely! Don't be too dry and serious.

Stay young! Youth is wild! Of all things to preserve as you grow older, save your IMAGINATION most of all! Dream! Fabricate! Fancy! Plan and promise! Look ahead, see ahead, be ahead! Use your imagination.

There's no need ever to grow old. Let your future always be bigger than your past or your present. That's the way to sell them—FOR YOU CAN ONLY SELL THEM WHILE YOU'RE YOUNG!

8. GROW—AND YOU CLICK!

No growth, no promise!

Be bigger today than you were yesterday!

Some important person may not have seen you for six months. He remembers how you were then. Unconsciously he is inspecting you today, to see if you have slipped or forged ahead. Actually *he is prejudiced toward the fact that you have slipped.* Most people slip as time goes by. You would have to be an exception to have gone ahead.

This shows how important it is that you acquire a little more of all the worth-while things as each new day arrives. A little more knowledge. A little more perspective. A little more skill. A little more freshness. A little more enthusiasm. A little more philosophy. A little more vision.

Grow! It is the worthiest form of promise and the surest way to protect promise. You grow if you simply make use of the time that is given to you. All men are alike in this regard that each is given twenty-four hours every day. If those hours are used for growth instead of pastime, your promise will increase as each day passes, and you will be a perpetual surprise to your friends, acquaintances and associates.

Remember, it's the rare man who doesn't slip as time passes. All who knew you or know you now are SURE

85

that you have slipped since they last met you. Let your daily plan of growth and the ever present buzz and bustle of an expanding personality furnish the ringing contradiction of this universal conviction.

9. SAY "YES" WITHOUT YOUR TONGUE IN YOUR CHEEK

Nobody can pile up a good score on the quality of promise, until he has posted himself as a willing man. Be willing! If someone asks you, "Will you do me a favor?" say "yes" without first asking what the favor is. Have a little faith—the person who phrases his request that way always asks for something it is easy to do. Surprise him by being generous, without restrictions.

That man has promise who will always answer yes to a request for an undescribed favor. The world figures he is rich.

The miracle of the willing attitude is that its larger benefits occur within you, rather than outside you. Of course, your willingness pleases others, and to please people is the height of practicality. But your willing attitude does more. It serves to create an immediate responsiveness on the part of all your own faculties. With a willing attitude you are sure to have plenty of pep. And the expenditures of energy that this willingness lets you in for, are restored in multiplied degree by that same willingness.

Be willing and you'll never be exhausted, or even tired. The man with energy to spare is unquestionably the man with promise.

10. NEVER SAY "NO"

If someone asks you if you will do something, whether that something is a feat of strength or skill or a simple selfish favor, don't say "No"—if you care anything about possessing the quality known as promise.

"No" may be the truthful answer and the only proper answer, but the man who sells himself never gives it. He says: "I'll do all I can; I'll look into it at once!"

He gives you the material which allows you to keep on hoping. That's promise!

To say "No" flatly is cruel, harsh. It unsells the other man on you. And it is never necessary to say it, unless he is a logical man and wants the truth, not false hope.

"No" closes the matter. And then there is no more promise. To keep the promise alive, keep the matter open forever, or at least as long as anyone is interested. You never have to turn down anyone on a favor he is seeking from you. If you can't grant it, you can surely postpone its rejection. When you delay in saying "No" to a request for a favor you can't give, something generally turns up which takes the supplicant off your trail. He gets what he wants through another means, he finds another job, his need no longer exists. And in stalling him politely, you have avoided offending him.

11. ALWAYS HAVE GOOD INTENTIONS

Have good intentions in your heart as well as on your lips. Your inner determination to bring good to all will

87

coat your actions with sparkle and expectation. Good intentions are positive; aiming at good is the promise of good. Questionable motives, or strategy involving harm or loss to others, obliterate all your promise.

12. THE BEST WAY TO CREATE PROMISE IS NOT TO PROMISE AT ALL

A promise *from* you means little promise *for* you.

A promise is a definite declaration that you will do a certain thing at a certain time. There's nothing exciting about that, nothing soft and wondrous. Your very declaration invites challenge, and if you fail to make good you have condemned yourself for all time.

The best promise is the promise you cause people to create in their own minds. If, in their enthusiasm, they promise too much for you, they, not you, are to blame. Let all errors concerning your capacity be someone else's; never your own.

13. BE A "BEAR FOR WORK"

Do many things and in great volume. Be able to start quickly and to work with speed, so that you can amaze others with your production. Use the hours of the night as well as the day to produce, and you will cause even greater amazement. After all, production is simply the sum total of all your applied minutes. Add *intensity* to all your production. A fertile brain and a tireless hand are two indelible marks of promise.

88

14. THROW AWAY YOUR HAMMER AND GET A HORN

To have promise you must be a true optimist. Your outlook is plus, positive. All you can see ahead is good. You continually point toward the good, you expect the good, evil or negative things have no place in your life.

Consequently, you're a booster. You push, praise, cheer for the good goal.

You can't be a knocker, a carping critic, and have promise. It is true many people like to partake in disparaging conversations and are constantly on the lookout for a partner who will criticize and find fault along with them. But that partner is a destructionist, not a man of promise.

When you're looking for something good to happen, you want to talk to the booster. His very presence seems to hurry the good, to make it more sure.

★

Guts

I wish I could use a word like "Courage" or "Nerve" or "Backbone" instead of the vulgar word GUTS.

But no goody-goody word can take the place of guts. It means something the other words don't mean—it describes a quality that is so important in establishing your individuality that it must be placed third on the list of essentials!

And Guts it must be—nothing else. You sometimes hear a man say of another in admiration: "He certainly has a lot of GUTS!" The man isn't saying: "He certainly has a lot of Courage" or "He certainly has a lot of Nerve." When he says Guts he means Guts.

Guts has a brashness, a coarseness, a ruthlessness and an ignorance to it. Guts has practical action where courage has merely theoretical existence. Guts goes into the selling fire and takes the order away while mere courage is making noble resolutions. Guts always wins!

The word "Guts" derives from that particular part of the anatomy generally associated with the stomach region.

It was probably first used to refer to a fighter who got a punch in the stomach and didn't quit.

The stomach region is the quitting region. A blow on the heart, too much strain on the lungs, a terrifying pain in the stomach, and the great temptation to quit assails you.

Anyone can fight when he's full of power and pep, in perfect wind, and health, and has all his strength.

But it takes a thoroughbred to continue when his muscles have about caved in, when his lungs are breaking, his wind is gone, and his heart is going to stop any second. But if he has guts, HE DOES CONTINUE!

The time to show your guts is when you get that terrible, sickening punch in the stomach.

The punch in the stomach, in a business way, may be merely a refusal to give you an order, a minor insult, ridicule, defeat, discouragement. You have the choice of fainting then or there, or of pulling yourself together and FIGHTING.

Build up that stomach region. Accept the hard knocks as necessary exercise. Welcome the abuse because it is toughening your muscles, giving you better wind, a stronger heart, and MORE GUTS.

Don't regard Guts merely as a work of character. View it in the bigger way, as a quality which is a versatile and practical instrument in selling yourself.

1. CARRY A PUNCH AND USE IT

Carry a punch with you. In everything you do let this punch, this force, this power and strength be visible.

An old-time counselor in worldly wisdom suggested "the iron hand under the velvet glove." The velvet glove calls for diplomacy, but diplomacy or no diplomacy, the iron hand must always be there if the world is to know you have guts. That's the important part of it! Not only must you have guts, but you must see to it that the world *knows* you have this quality.

Cultivate a voice that is loud enough to be heard, strong enough to cause a volume of vibration that immediately draws attention to you. You don't have to scream to be heard. But you can put the punch in your voice that makes people stop and listen.

Show the strong side, the plus side always. There is nothing to apologize for, so don't apologize! Deal in the positive only—never be negative. Move fast, without hesitation. Flare up once in a while—get "mad!" Never compromise. Never stop until your issue comes to a conclusion: you can't let it hang fire, be shelved, mislaid or forgotten. Drive through with it while it is up for consideration; it's the boat and you're the captain, and you have to take your ship into port, you can't let it rest even for a day out in the middle of the sea.

The punch you put behind your work, and your issues, will give them an importance that commands the respect and cooperation of all concerned. They just *have* to be settled and settled *your* way!

2. DON'T ASK THE BOSS IF IT'S ALL RIGHT WITH HIM

Initiative and radium are a great deal alike. They are both exceedingly rare, yet a mere drop of either will rock the world.

"He's worth his weight in radium," George Ade once said of a man he admired. And friends of yours can just as sincerely say of you (if you merit it), "He's worth his weight in *initiative!*"

Initiative is your ability *to begin something*. To begin it, without being told by someone else. To start the job entirely on your own responsibility without asking anyone else to share the hazards with you. If you have initiative, you are not afraid to let others steal the fruits of your work if it is successful; but principally, you are not afraid to take the entire blame for it, *if it fails!*

Nobody with initiative ever embarrasses himself. Try as you may, you can't think of anyone who ever made a fool of himself by starting the ball rolling. The man with initiative CAN fail and DOES fail, but failure doesn't stop him because his initiative lifts him up after the fall and helps him win on the next attempt.

Thus the magic force of initiative is praised everywhere. Organizations laud it. Business loves it. Even the angels whoop it up when they see a lone man step out of the beaten path to do something he isn't supposed to do, doesn't have to do, wasn't told to do. He does it merely because he thinks it's about time somebody did it! The best reason of all!

You've some time waited in a long line while a huge

crowd of people—all full grown, all sane and intelligent —tried to crowd out of a church or hall or building through a doorway that was only half open. While burning up with the stupidity of the delay, you still suffered as the crowd slowly pushed out. Then suddenly a man behind you, who didn't believe in waiting or wasting time, left his place at the end, walked briskly to the half of the doorway that was blocked, and without hesitation or uncertainty pushed the other half of the door open, *and walked out!* Instantly the mob followed, saying: "Why didn't somebody do that before?" *You* had had the same idea while you waited, but you *waited.* The man with initiative didn't wait. He did a sensible thing, a necessary thing, straightforwardly and bravely. The herd follows the leader because—well, because it *has* to follow initiative.

If initiative is so miraculous, why not use it? It isn't a *foreign* subject with you. You *think* a lot of things, you *plan* a lot of things, you *see the need* for a lot of things.

Yet you are afraid to "stick your neck out." Don't *be* that way! Take initiative as your shield and you'll never get hurt! Take initiative as your food and your table will be bountifully spread! Take initiative as your book and you'll be the most educated of men! Initiative will lead you into verdant pastures, the life of courage and freedom, the proper destiny of the *individual.*

Be not like dumb, driven cattle—be a man with initiative. Start something! Try something! Do something! And don't ask mama, the boss, or the man on the street if it will be all right. Just *ask yourself* and if it seems sensible, reasonable and necessary, follow your instincts and *do it*. The ability to act as an individual independent of all others is the thing that makes you a *person*—it's the main reason for your existence, the mainspring of your whole life. You *have* this ability— use it, and it becomes the most irresistible of all human forces, that river of radium, INITIATIVE!

3. THE SLAVE DRIVER'S TOUCH

The "ag" in "aggressive" stands for the Latin preposition "at," "to," or "toward."

It's the key to the quality! *At* him, Mister! Bring the fight *toward* him, *to* him.

The attack and the control of the fighting side are the essence of aggressiveness. You take the fight to the other man before he brings it to you. A good offense is the first step in self-protection—and you have no time to get afraid while you're on the offensive.

Force yourself continuously. Complete power to develop aggressiveness lies with you, no one else. All you have to do is "get after yourself." Give yourself a good pushing around from the moment you wake up until the moment you drop off to sleep.

Be your own boss, and be a HARD boss, a slave driver. You can't put too much push behind yourself, and with this push ever active, there will be scarcely anything that you can't push over!

Day-by-day practice of aggressiveness soon produces

96

those traits which are commonly known as "cockiness" and "gumption." Bearing these labels, nobody is going to step on you. Nor are you ever going to be found sleeping on the job, or resting on your seat of wisdom. You will be constantly on the go, a stimulation and an inspiration for all people, because gumption inspires gumption and the inspired audience pays dutiful respect to the source of the inspiration!

BE BOLD "OUT LOUD"

When trouble comes, when pain, misery, and distress surround you, you find that nothing gives you better support or greater consolation than a bold heart. You and YOUR COURAGE are bigger than all your adversities put together. Such an attitude never fails to pull you through.

Assert yourself *by being bold!* Publish your boldness, say OUT LOUD the courageous, daring things that declare your fortitude and your determination. By publishing your boldness in the hour of greatest danger you give courage to others, some of which courage is wafted right back to you. The sound of your own voice, its ringing spirit, and the meaning of the bold words you say all will combine to fix your resolution and steady your nerve.

4. STAND ON YOUR OWN FEET

The man with Guts is a decisive man; his outlines are cleanly cut, his personality is easily brought into focus.

97

Behind this clean-cut outline stands the element of strength—the man with guts is a strong man.

Now strength isn't necessarily physical size, for generally small people have more guts than large people. Nor is it mental or intellectual prowess for oftentimes our greatest geniuses are shy, timid souls afraid of their own shadows. Strength is a fine combination of spirit, of egotism, of selfishness, of will power that emanates entirely from your ego.

In order to be strong all you have to do is *decide* to be strong! Right now you have plenty of guts; all you have to do is lift the barrier and go into action.

You are ready to match blow for blow. In the presence of another of higher rating than you, you still remain normal. You answer strength with strength. You show the plus side, the forceful side always. Your every sentence, gesture, is accented with emphasis and decision. You cut away from all alliances, you stand "on your own."

There is nothing so beautiful, nothing so glorious as to see a man stand on his own feet, rely for help on no other person or thing, face and conquer dreadful opposition through sheer force of personality and inherent strength. As soon as you learn to get by single handed, without the aid of any other person or persons, in that very moment you begin to *believe in yourself!*

The power to conquer all obstacles is right inside yourself. *Decide now* to use of this very power instead of trying to figure whom you can get to help you over the trying stretch in the road.

5. "IGNORANT NERVE" COMES IN HANDY

The whole world seems to condemn "ignorant nerve." Why? Maybe because we are quick to condemn those things which we envy in others.

The main trick in developing guts—provided you're missing at present on this desirable quality—is the magic word *ignore*.

Observe the man with guts. Does he stop and weigh all considerations of a subject or a situation before he goes into action? Does he appraise his own side carefully to see if he is out of order? Does he worry about offending other people, trespassing on certain rights of theirs, "stepping on their toes"?

No! The Man with Guts breaks in, totally ignoring the consequences of his act. He simply, crudely, almost brutally, brings the situation under his own control, undoes the hours, even months, of careful planning and maneuvering by others who go about things in a round-about way.

After all, ignorance is refreshing! It stimulates by its directness, it relieves by cutting away a mass of red tape.

Ignore! Ignore what others will think of you! Ignore the consequences of the step you are now taking! Ignore any weak consideration of whether the time is right or wrong. Ignore the need or foundation for the step you are taking!

Go ahead and confront the man! Start your plan! Chase caution out of your house. Ignore everybody and everything that might prevent you from taking the step or even delaying it. Ignore and GET GUTS!

6. "I'M GOING HOME FOR SUPPER WITH MA AND PA!"

You're not afraid when you go home to eat supper in the kitchen with your Ma and Pa. A million contacts, unlimited affection, have made them and you so perfectly acquainted that you know no new situation may arise of which you'll get frightened.

But say you've made an appointment with an important man to meet him at a very ritzy hotel for lunch. You've never been inside this hotel before, and you are completely awed by its reputation.

A thousand fears come into your heart as you prepare to keep the appointment. What's the right door to go into? Should you notice the liveried doorman or will he notice you and make you present credentials for entering? Where inside the lobby should you take your hat off or, on the other hand, should you keep it on and not look like a farmer? Which way to turn for the elevator, the desk, or the spot where the man said he would meet you? Won't it be apparent to everybody that you —you big dumb yokel—have never been inside this place before (and everybody else in town comes here every day)? Aren't you doomed to making a hundred mistakes before you even get your bearings?

These are your thoughts—but they shouldn't be your thoughts.

Your thoughts should be: "I'm going home to eat

supper with my Ma and Pa! I've been through this a thousand times—nothing new can happen here!"

This attitude of being immune to strangers or strange situations, this total disregard for all the UNKNOWN or UNEXPECTED has a name. It is called POISE. Poise is the deliberate shunting aside of all fears arising from new and uncontrollable circumstances.

What you are actually afraid of *never happens!* Many of the things that might truly give you some uneasiness never come into your mind at all, simply because fear is so impractical. The fears you suffer are wild, foolish, dreamy, ethereal, stupid, non-feasible, impossible to justify by the mechanics of human nature or everyday existence. Some things perhaps should be feared; but these you blindly ignore anyway. So why not ignore them all?

In the new situation simply say: "I've done this thing a thousand times before. I'm merely going home to eat supper with my Ma and Pa. Everything will be O.K."

7. "I SAW HIM FIRST!"

This situation was made for human conquest—so you be the conqueror. The most consistent quality a man can possess is selfishness. Never apologize for being selfish —never pull your punches when it comes to exerting your selfishness.

The true selfish attitude—the point of view that distinguishes the man who has guts, is this: *He views every situation as if it belongs to him!*

Face to face with a strange problem, a scary task, an uncertain development, just say to yourself: "This is my job, my man, my answer, my territory: THE WHOLE THING BELONGS TO ME!" Then step in and take it!

Modesty, bashfulness, self-effacement have nothing in common with Guts. Conscious and admitted selfishness is the controlling principle of guts. Be proud to be selfish!

To be truly selfish you must know your *objective*. This is the thing you're after, the thing you want, and you'll let nothing interfere with your getting it. Singleness of purpose and a single-track mind are necessary here, to drive your selfishness home to its natural conclusion.

And if something gets in your way, you'll ruthlessly push it aside. If you're going to sell a big contract, that is the thing that must go over, come what may. If you lack ruthlessness in executing the means that help you attain your end, you might as well have no objective at all, for in every attempt to achieve anything important, there always enters a sentimental reason for stopping. The selfish drive furnishes the momentum to keep proceeding in the face of all resistance.

8. STICK TO YOUR GUNS

Hardly anything succeeds on the first attempt; a thing must be tried, must be done, many times before it actually goes over.

Why then let the criterion of your success be: Do I fail or do I succeed on the first attempt? If this is your criterion, you'll nearly always fail.

All those who have won any contest or any cause know that victory came after a long series of discouragements and failures. Perseverance won.

Nobody can ever defeat the man who sticks to his guns.

Just look back on your own successes and recall how they came. Didn't nearly every one of them follow a series of failures? By repeating the failures often enough you finally hit on the right way to succeed. To have complete success all you need is one success; and even though a thousand failures precede that victory, the victory will be just as sweet or even sweeter on account of the failures.

Perseverance can be blind—and then it's glorious. The fighting cock, the battling bulldog, know only one thing—to hang on forever. If death comes while they're persevering, then they die a glorious death. But generally merely by hanging on, you'll win, for the other man will get tired before you do.

Cultivate this *blind* perseverance. Never give up! Not even for death itself!

Cultivate *conscious* perseverance, too. It's artificial but just as effective. Consciously convince yourself that failure is to be expected, that there is no substitution for endless repetition of the same effort. Deliberately set about chalking up the necessary number of failures before you even dream of success. With this attitude, you can never doubt the success that will ultimately be yours.

Perseverance is the one quality of courage that the other man recognizes and respects in you more than any other.

When you were a child you used to play "it" with other boys. Some of the boys could run much faster than others and were therefore always safe and daring in their movements, teasing and baiting the one who was "it" and defying him to catch them. If in the group there was one determined "it" player, one persistent, single-track mind, who, when made "it," started after the nearest boy to him, whether known to be slow or fast, and prepared to follow him steadfastly, even while lagging far behind, for minutes, and even hours, the fast runner soon gave up. He knew the boy with perseverance would catch him eventually, so he decided to be "it" to get rid of the annoyance. Everybody gives in to the one who perseveres.

Once you are known as a man who sticks to your guns, the other party will always give in early in the game, just to avoid the rigors of a contest that can have only one ending—victory for you.

Perseverance feeds your courage—for perseverance is nothing but an automatic second-by-second renewal of courage. There can be no real fear in the heart of the man who won't quit.

In most things you do, there always comes a time when the burdens and apparent futility of the task dismay you—that's the time to keep on working! For just as surely as those dismaying periods occur, there also occur stretches when everything favors you, when you get the unexpected breaks. At this point crowd your luck! Press forward to take full advantage of the breaks, but the important thing to remember is that these "lucky stretches" will SURELY appear if you only carry on through the bad stretches.

Finish what you start. To quit a job half done is to disgrace yourself in your own eyes and in the eyes of the world. Nobody has any use for a quitter.

9. ALWAYS CARRY A BANK ROLL

Money is not almighty but you can do more with it than with any other single thing in your repertory. How essential that you always have some with you—not necessarily to spend—but to give you that feeling of safety and reinforcement which in many a situation turns into real courage.

There are many men who go to work every day with just enough money in their pockets to pay for their carfare and their lunch. They make no provision for the unexpected occurrence or circumstance which may demand that they produce money or suffer immediate embarrassment.

If a dollar is all you carry with you, you soon become known as a one-dollar man. You may not admit that you are always light on the currency, but your friends and associates soon become conscious of it. When you have to hold back, dodge the issue, prove reluctant to spend, your financial situation is as public as the public debt. Your lack of cash is nothing more than lack of punch, of guts.

Of course, if you have no money anywhere, you have every right to be financially embarrassed. But if you have cash, you can carry at least fifty dollars with you at all times. It certainly isn't too much to risk and neither is it too much to have for the unexpected emergency.

Carrying the money gives you a feeling of power and gains the respect of your friends. For, though all you spend is a half dollar, somehow or other the people who are nearby when you change even the smallest bill know whether you carry real money with you or are just getting by with your carfare and lunch allotment.

You don't tell, and you don't show them the money, but your manner of conducting yourself in all financial situations is such that they know you have backing. Your lack of scariness, your ease and composure, are the result of the money in your pocket; that is what people see and that is what gives you a heavier score in the guts column!

10. RISE TO YOUR FULL HEIGHT

If you would have guts, you simply must keep cool! Steady!

With all this excitement in the air, with all these unusual circumstances surrounding you, you are very likely to start vibrating.

Steady! Keep cool. A good trick when you feel your
nerves starting to tingle is to rise to your full height or
if you are sitting lift your head as high in the air as
you can, as if you were trying to see over the heads of
a crowd. That's the very idea! Keep your head. See
over the crowd and over the unusual circumstances
which tempt you to blow up. Survey the situation
calmly, and dispassionately. Measure it as you would
a motionless wall, floor or piece of land.

Nervousness is an admission to others and, more
seriously, to yourself, that you are afraid. Keep cool!

11. THE OTHER MAN IS JUST AS SCARED AS YOU ARE

Take heart! Because you are afraid, you needn't feel
so alone. Practically everybody in that big gathering
is just as scared as you are.

To distinguish yourself as the man who is not afraid,
all you have to do is SHOW A LITTLE LESS FEAR THAN
THE OTHERS.

For Guts is nothing more or less than not being quite
as scared as the ordinary person.

The other man is just as scared as you are. But get
out of his class; it's easy to rise above the ordinary level
of fear and carry yourself as if you have no fear at all.

12. THEY DON'T CARE ABOUT YOU

Your timidity is based on this ridiculous assumption:
That people care about you enough even to notice you.

Once and for all let this truth sink in: THEY DON'T CARE ABOUT YOU. Since your fears are based on their caring, and they don't care, your fears have no substance or justification.

How many ridiculous things did you notice in other people in the last twenty-four hours? Quick! Write them down—if you can. If you did notice anything out of the way, the chances are it was some fault that particularly annoyed you, probably because you yourself were also guilty of it in some form.

Those people as they passed within the scope of your notice feared *your* opinions, *your* remarks, *your* ridicule—and all the while you were totally unconscious that they were thinking about anything!

Even now you can hardly believe that another should even think for a minute whether you care a bit if his tie is straight, or whether the pin stripe on his shirt is too pronounced, or if you're going to notice the new pair of shoes he is breaking it. Silly, isn't it? And isn't it just as silly, when *you* have the same fears and trepidations concerning other people's opinions of *you?*

Rout that timidity! The only thing you should be afraid of is timidity itself. For timidity gives you an awkwardness, a fumbling of control, a lack of direction which seriously hampers all your movements. When you are afraid, you're below par, and you always should be at par in order to make a showing in the competitive strife of the world.

Act quickly before you have time to get scared. It's the preliminary brooding over the matter that weakens your decision. The more time spent in contemplating the thing you are afraid of makes it that much harder to overcome. Jump in and do it quickly!

Force yourself to do the thing by committing yourself to a course of action from which you can't withdraw. If you're backward about taking a suit downtown to be altered, postpone that decision, simply put the suit in the box and resolve merely to take the box downtown. Carrying the box downtown will just about force you to take it into the store to have the suit fixed, for you can't be encumbered carrying that box all around the city all day long.

Do the thing often enough, get intimate with it! Familiarity breeds contempt—of fear. The better you know a thing, the less reason you see why you should ever be afraid of it.

Act the opposite of the way you feel! You feel timid —act bold! Merely assuming the bold role, helps rout most of the timidity.

Put your money into the thing. Perhaps the easiest way to force yourself into an enterprise that requires daring, forwardness, and guts on your own part, is to invest money in the thing before you call on yourself to furnish the guts. You may buy equipment. Pay dues. Layout preliminary expenditures. You will then consider it a crime to see that money go to waste unused, and force yourself to do the thing that you fear. When your money is in the thing or the enterprise, it gets a great deal more support from your end.

When you're feeling particularly sensitive, backward,

shy, or frightened, two instincts move you: First, to run away; second, to seek help. Running away only makes you more timid—advance, never retreat, in the face of fear!

And seek *no help from anyone*—inside yourself is all the stuff necessary to rout fear! Act *solo*.

You and you alone have the power to rout your own timidity.

Know this finally, you can be full of timidity—and still have plenty of GUTS. It's the worthy man, the great man, who no matter how scared he is of real or imaginary danger, STILL ACTS courageously and unflinchingly while distraught with temptations to run away or quit. That's guts!

13. YOU HAVE ONLY ONE PERSON TO ACCOUNT TO

Have only one person to account to—yourself. Practically all fear of ridicule is based on the foolish premise that you will have to account to someone else for your queer, weak, or futile actions. A mistake! First of all those other people don't care whether you're a clown or a wise man, they don't think about you at all. If they did, why worry about them anyhow? They are not a part of you, they share none of your ambitions or desires, they have no stake whatsoever in your actions. There is no one to account to on the outside, but inside is the final judge and arbiter of your acts, your own conscience and self-respect.

Most of the things you plan get the internal O.K.

which should be all you need to go into action. But after
you decide a thing is all right to do, you stop, falter,
and quake, as you consider what others will say of you.
That bugaboo "what others will say" has killed more
enterprise and initiative than all other fears and obstacles put together.

Don't care what others will say, pay attention to
yourself—WHAT DO YOU SAY? You need only account
to yourself for the things you try to do, and even if you
fail to do them, you'll preserve your own self-respect by
having tried. When you don't try, you certainly have
no chance to win, and every such withdrawal is a severe
blow to your self-respect.

☆
_____

SECTION 4

Approach

Approach is the art of making contacts.

Every time you can make a contact, make it.

If there's a meeting tonight which you are invited to attend, but you feel so tired, hungry and dirty, you want to go home, go to the meeting anyway! There will be a lot of men there you don't know, but should.

Every time you can make a contact, make it!

The simplest and lightest form of contact is, "How do you do, Mr. Jones, pleased to meet you!" But that's hardly a contact at all. To make it a real contact, you have to do something for Jones.

Because the only thing that can cause Jones to remember you or want to deal with you in the future is the fact that *the contact also means something to him!*

So be sure to deliver some service to Jones. You must be willing to vote for him. To put in a good word for

113

him. To do anything that causes him to gain a net advantage as a direct result of the contact. This way you sew him up. A good contact calls for reciprocal action.

You must care about Jones before Jones will care about you! To care about him you have to want to please him, you have to pay more than ordinary attention to him. Study his personality, listen with great attention while he speaks. Even a partial application of this principle will make a deep impression on Jones, because he isn't in the habit of having anybody pay much attention to him.

If Jones were a really big man, whose favor would mean a fortune to you, and you had the chance to contact him you certainly would do all these things. That is, YOU THINK so now. But you wouldn't know the best way to pull it off, unless you had a background of unlimited practice on contacts that were apparently useless and insignificant. But no contact is useless or insignificant! Cultivate every acquaintance however slight. Pay attention to the man. Make yourself like him. Do all you can to please him. This sort of practice will develop a marvelous approach faculty in yourself, and not one single item of the practice will be wasted, for you will find that every one of these "minor" contacts will soon be paying you dividends.

1. CONNECTIONS

Connections are not built up all at once. It's a slow process, but not too slow if you make a regular procedure out of it. Study and cultivation make them grow.

They first start in childhood play. Then at school—grammar, high, and college. Neighborhood activity, church activity, lodge and social work add more. Sports make still more. But the biggest gold mine of all is business.

Whatever job you're in, right there is your biggest opportunity for making connections. Make it your business to know *of* every authority in your field, then make it your business to *know* the authority either personally or by correspondence.

No matter how obscure the desk at which you sit, that desk is a gold mine. Think of the salesmen who call on you. Each man is another connection—and in addition ALL his connections can also be yours, if you ask for them.

The timid bookkeeper who "doesn't know a single soul" may go to accounting school at night, make a friend of the teacher, and find the same teacher willing to deliver to him any or all of his connections.

It's a funny thing about connections. People like to deliver them to you. They somehow know that unless they work these connections every once in a while, they may get rusty and useless. So they give them a workout even when there is absolutely nothing in it for them. It somehow gives them a feeling of power to draw on their large acquaintanceship in your behalf.

Though you build up your own connections slowly, and require several years to pass before you may honestly say you "have a host of friends," it is well to realize that you actually don't need *many* connections to have *a lot* of connections. Be nervy enough to ask your present connections to deliver all the connections they have individually to you when the occasion may require such delivery.

2. IF YOU WOULD PERCOLATE, CIRCULATE!

The secret of making connections is *circulate*.

You can't meet people by retiring to your study, your cloister, or your hermitage. Circulate. Get out in the world where people are and meet them there. Join as many organizations and associations as you appropriately can and become active in all of them. You don't have to burden yourself with a lot of detailed work, don't even have to take any of the offices that will quickly be offered to you, but you can take a real interest in every activity, serve on committees, attend meetings and events where many people gather. You will soon get to know a lot of people, make many friends and useful acquaintances.

But you have to be there actually, *with your body*. They've got to see you, hear you, feel your physical personality if they are ever to remember you.

Most successful men are "joiners." They belong to clubs, to organizations, to organized movements concerned with bettering the community or the particular trade or activity to which they belong.

Circulate. Go there. Regularly! Join! Become active! It's apparently non-productive work and that's why you are cutting down on it now, but actually it will bear fruit a hundredfold in getting you acquainted with the people who really count and who can introduce or help you to meet the person or persons you want to meet for any special service.

8. THE LIST TO WHICH YOU SEND CHRISTMAS CARDS

You, though you wonder on first thought who they are, have a lot of connections. Everybody has.

All you have to do is sit down and figure. Count the people you know and those who know you. Start with your intimate family, your father and mother, your sisters and brothers. Take your in-laws, too. Take your intimate friends. Take the people you associate with every day in business. These along with your neighbors, your schoolmates, and very special contacts—notice how they coincide with the list of people to whom you send Christmas cards—offer a wealth of material for making any contact possible.

Supposing you would like to interview a certain man, and on first consideration, he seems a difficult man to meet. Don't give up. Start to figure. You don't know him, but whom do you know who may know him? Again you say: "Nobody! There's no connection at all!"

Were you ever on hand when three or four people in a group decided that a certain man was to be approached, and nobody knew him? Did you notice how they figured and figured and without the slightest uncertainty a way presented itself to make meeting the man possible? Sometimes it's a very remote connection; sometimes it's an obvious one and an intimate one. But the connection is always there if you will only seek it.

We have no fear or difficulty in approaching our real friends. We call them up, drop into their offices, write them letters. But the man we have never met before stops us cold. It shouldn't be. He has some intimate friend or associate to whom he owes a debt; there's someone somewhere who can approach him with ease and safety. That someone is related to you somehow, directly or indirectly. To make the meeting possible all you have to do is *think and try.*

You think of someone you are not afraid to contact and ask him if he knows the man you want to meet. He doesn't, but in order to help you, he may know of someone who can swing it, or he may think of an idea for the meeting that you have ignored. At any rate, the attempt at the meeting brings you closer to its culmination. Every man whose aid you enlist helps push you closer to the desired end. It can't fail.

You can figure out any kind of meeting or interview and set the stage in advance so that you go in highly recommended and honored, and sure of an appreciative audience. Think and try!

4. BE NICE TO HIS SECRETARY

The big man is rather easy to see. Call on him.

You may not get in to see him on your first call, but you certainly will be able to meet and speak with his secretary. The secretary is there for just that purpose. She waits on all callers. She decides on the urgency of the interview, and it is well to treat her with a great deal of courtesy and deference. Her friendship is most valuable in creating the right impression for you and in causing her to find a generous amount of time for your interview with her boss.

Your right to the interview may be only mild, but if you really want it and can so impress the secretary—through honest statement and consistent follow-up—the interview will have to ensue.

5. NEVER RESIST THE BUYER WHO WANTS TO DO YOU A FAVOR

In your relations with the other man, there eventually comes a time when he seeks to help you. This is a natural expression of his masculine complex; he wants to display his strength, his power. In the favor he bestows upon you, he wishes to extend himself and live in your memory.

Let him! By all means let him! Under no circumstances resist the man who is trying to do you the favor.

Of course, he is thinking primarily of himself and not of you. Of course, he expects you to applaud his action mightily and remain everlastingly in his debt. Accept these responsibilities. For by owing him a return favor, you must be given further chance to contact him. By being forced to become grateful, you are handed a permanent pass to contact him at any time, in order once more to voice your gratitude. A perfect set-up!

In looking for something from the man, you are too prone to regard yourself as first having the duty of doing something for him before you can ever expect anything in return. This is not always the case. Sometimes the other surprises you and attempts to be the donor instead of the receiver. Do not be caught napping. Accept his favors and with them receive the further opportunity of contacting him for the rest of his life.

6. START A BANK ACCOUNT OF NEW FRIENDS AND ACQUAINTANCES

That contacts are valuable you cannot deny. How shall you go about making contacts, acquiring this valuable property?

Start a bank account!

This account will receive only the names of new people you have never met before, people of good standing, particularly business people. You will not deposit a name—a contact—in this account till you can honestly prove to yourself that it *is* a contact. There are simple rules for determining when a casual contact really becomes a true contact, which is nothing more than a friendship or an acquaintanceship.

Set an objective for your saving plan. Say that in the next year you are going to make at least 100 new contacts. You are going to "make friends" with 100 people of importance, persons you have never met before. You are starting from scratch because that's the way a good bank account starts. A clean break-away!

Get your bank book, too, a little book in which you write down the names, *after* they have received the rating of a true contact!

Just think—100 new acquaintances to be made in the next 365 days. Sounds like a pretty tall order, doesn't it? The chances are you haven't made many more than 100 true contacts in your entire life. Then how are you going to make 100 in a single year?

That's the beauty of a bank account. When you're out to save money, you REALLY DO SAVE IT, save it with surprising ease and speed. It's all in making a *definite drive.*

You've really got to hump if you're going to average about ONE new friend every third day of the year. You're going to have to double up—make several friends at a time! You're going to appear in places where you can meet people—you are not going to expect them to come to you!

How do you do it exactly?

You receive a notice of a meeting that's going to be held. You're invited. Ordinarily you wouldn't go. Now you decide that you will go, for a meeting is a place where you meet people, and you have to meet a lot of people to make those 100 contacts in a year!

You may sit down at a table with a bunch of strangers. Nobody has introduced you (in fact, each man at the table is conscious of the fact that nobody has introduced HIM).

What do you do? Since nobody speaks up, and since

you've got to deposit some fresh names in your bank book, YOU speak up. You introduce yourself. When the other man tells you his name, YOU LISTEN. You have to write that name down in your book (provided you can develop him into a true contact) and you have to know exactly how to spell it! Imagine! For the first time in your life, probably, you are paying attention to people's names! Do they like it? Well, do you like it when another man muffs *your* name, and don't you like it much better when he shows he cares about getting it *straight?*

You also have to find out who the man is, what he does, where he works, what special interests he has, in order to prepare to develop him into a true contact.

Automatically you find yourself being nice to the man, and the man finds you're being nice. He hasn't had so much honest attention (an interest in the mechanical facts about him is HONEST ATTENTION) paid to him in a long time, and he likes it. He warms to you. At once you have laid the groundwork for a more personal visit with him in the near future.

The proper kind of first meeting always prepares for the follow-up. This follow-up may be a letter, a personal call, a date for lunch, an attendance at a game or sport event, or a walk together outdoors, or another apparently chance meeting. The extra cordiality put into the first meeting is bound to draw the two of you together later. Future contacts disclose a mutuality of interest, you find you like the same things, and you like each other's company.

In your attempt to turn the casual contact into a true and permanent contact, you go out of your way to do favors for your new acquaintance. Out of these favors inevitably issues the result you desire—a permanent contact.

Now you are able to write a new name down in your bank book, a deposit of incalculable value in selling yourself. Your future is growing!

7. KEEP UP WITH YOUR OLD FRIENDS AND ACQUAINTANCES

What good is it to pile up a flock of fine friends and acquaintances, and let them die off?

Keep in touch with them! Leaving out the matter of sentiment entirely—a matter which, incidentally, should never be left out—just consider your acquaintances as your personal property. If you don't renew your friendships and contacts and keep them alive constantly, you are going to have a great depreciation charge, and pretty soon the property will be worth nothing to you.

It took time, expense, fortunate circumstance, and good feeling to bring you together with these people in the first place. Now that you've got them, be sure they are still friendly. Do them a favor every once in a while. Write them a letter. Arrange to bump into them by going to places where you suppose they will be. Visit with them! You know them—they know you—your next meeting is as easy as it is to work the nearest telephone.

123

If you have nothing to ask from these old friends, don't let the friendship grow rusty on that account. See if they have anything to ask from you. It's always easier to save a contact by doing something for the other person than by asking some favor from him.

Keep in touch. Use the same means for keeping up with old friends and acquaintances as you used in finding them originally.

From the standpoint of business, it's good business. From the standpoint of sentiment, it more than becomes you as a gentleman, a comrade, a warm, living, human being.

8. THE BETTER THE CONNECTION, THE LESS YOU SHOULD USE IT

If among your connections, you know one or two really big men, men of power and position, don't hurt your standing with those men by constantly calling on them for help. Don't drag in the BIG connection on a LITTLE thing. It is better to let the little thing spoil, from lack of connection, than force your big friend in. For if he likes to aid you at all he likes to aid you *well*, in something where his size and strength really count, and not in some picayunish affair that a much smaller man could swing. SAVE that big connection. Use it only in the last emergency. Your big friend will rate you much higher than the multitude of his other friends and acquaintances, who are constantly annoying him with trivial requests. Then when you need him in something REALLY BIG, you know he will be there.

TEN TIPS ON APPROACH

1. Develop an "approach personality." Carry yourself, speak and act, as if you assume your desires for the meeting will be granted; this reduces the power of the grantor to say "no." Avoid negatives or alternatives in presenting your proposition. The man of "approach personality" is always well-dressed, has a clear, steady voice, and looks too important to be ignored or refused.

2. Make a list. Make a list of the names of all the people who can mean something to you in the particular sphere in which you're operating. Have their addresses and their phone numbers, and a note concerning mutual acquaintances. Make it your business, through a steady plan of follow-up eventually to become friendly with them. You can't get them all at once, but you can bring every single one of them into your camp eventually.

3. Get a reputation. Your own ability to approach and connect up with people depends to a good extent on your reputation. Get a rep! Be known for quality work, honest and sportsmanlike dealings, and as a man of great promise. What you build up into your own reputation offers the other person a real reason for caring to deal with you.

4. Hire the best talent. Be sure that those who work for you have great skill and talent, more than you yourself possess. Never be afraid of talent, thinking it may undermine and unseat you in your business or social position. Talent is your best friend. As you associate

125

with and use skill, your own ability expands, and the effects of your activities offer a definite means of making many new profitable connections.

5. Write plenty of letters. You may hate to write letters, especially those which require a little creative thinking, but don't dodge this task. Write plenty of letters! Letters that aren't just in answer to other letters, cold matter-of-fact things, but letters that are a voluntary expression of congratulation, encouragement, or sentimental memory. PUT THE SENTIMENT IN! Such a daily letter writing program is bound to result in a world of friends.

6. Study the approach methods of others. Not everybody is easy to see; sometimes you, yourself, are unapproachable. Every once in a while, when you have to turn down someone who is trying to see you, stop and try to figure what you would do were you in the shoes of the person refused. Maybe you can think of something he forgot or discover the flaw in his approach technique.

7. Put yourself in the shoes of the man you're trying to approach. If you were he, how would you feel with all these people trying to crash his gate? He suspects, he KNOWS, that every one of you has selfish motives in trying to see him. Frame your approach in such a way that you clearly show your motive in seeing him is unselfish.

8. Know the big shots. To be an eventual big shot yourself, you must make it your business to know the big shots in your particular world. Suggestions: (a)

Write them letters, so they can see your name spelled out and can therefore remember it more readily sometime in the future. (b) Go where they make speeches; listen to their speeches; step up after they're through and congratulate them personally. In the flush of stimulation following a public performance no man has any resistance to approach. The same day you congratulate the man personally, write him a letter repeating the congratulatory sentiment. (c) Develop something he can use, a service, a bureau, a propaganda weapon that can be valuable to him. Extol him impersonally, for example, in a written article addressed to a different class of readers. Somehow or other, see that a clipping of the article reaches him.

9. Any contact is a good contact. Today's office boy may be tomorrow's president; make friends with him today. The information clerk, the receptionist, the switchboard operator, the assistant secretary, the secretary, can all be active aides in getting an interview and making a connection. Treat them with politeness and pleasantness and thank them profusely for the little things they do for you.

10. Learn how to go over a man's head. Sometimes you run into a stonewall in the person of a man who irrevocably refuses to deal with you. If you must get in, you MUST; so now proceed to go "over his head." Never threaten. Ask for permission to see someone subordinate to him, then try and sell that subordinate and in your interview with him seek to learn the lay of the land. Find out some other important man in the outfit, who has leisure and disposition for seeing people. Stretch your little contact as far as it will go. Quickly the "hard-to-see" man will hear of your maneuvers and invite you in to see him. Never try to excuse yourself for what you have done, but give him the impression you realized that he was altogether too busy for you to bother him.

★

Diplomacy

Diplomacy is the art of using people, things, issues and events to serve your own purpose. It is of two kinds.

First, *visible* diplomacy. The visible diplomat is always doing things for people, making himself agreeable, never rubbing their fur the wrong way. He's a pleaser.

Second, *invisible* diplomacy. This is, of course, the deeper side of the art. The practitioner of invisible diplomacy uses his people without ever letting them know they are being used. He is skilled in trading, compromise, finesse, opportunism. Many people succeed strictly through their ability at invisible diplomacy. If you would sell yourself to others, a good degree of competency in this art is absolutely essential.

If you are a person of spirit and guts, your diplomacy may be weak. Take care to strengthen it at once!

Visible Diplomacy

1. WHEN HE BORES YOU WITH A LONG-WINDED STORY

The key to all diplomacy is patience. Wait! Bide your
time! Let things work themselves out!

As soon as you try to hurry a situation along you
take the reins away from the man you're trying to sell
—a very undiplomatic act. If he is boring you with a
long-winded story, or raving about his kids instead of
coming to the point of business you are there to discuss,
suffer, suffer, suffer.

Do the thing the way he wants to do it—not the way
you want it done, not the way it should, by rights, be
done. The way *he* wants to do it is the *right* way.

Take your time—realizing that patience is the key
to diplomatic success, that the snail's pace at which you
are traveling now is really the fastest time in which the
deal can be consummated, and that all intermediate de-
lays, discouragements, distractions, or setbacks are stepping stones to your final success.

The faintest sign of impatience on your part destroys
your role of diplomat. Be patient and your diplomacy
will surely bear fruit!

2. ARE YOU A LITTLE BIT "OFF"?

When the children are a little bit "off," lacking in their
usual color, pep, and glow of life, the doctor prescribes
a *tonic* to set them up right again.

You were worried about the children at seeing them so listless, so unlike their usual selves. Their lack of *tone* made a grave difference in their health, you thought.

Do you ever think about your own lack of tone and realize that the impression you are making on other people may be exactly like the sick condition in your own children? Those other people, not being related to you, aren't going to worry about you and call in a doctor. It's a condition you have to fix up all by yourself! And it's serious. If you haven't tone, you've broken the circuit that allows you to reach others, that aids you in your diplomatic maneuvers aimed at swaying them.

Tone—that glow of life, bursting from inside you and aimed at soothing, pleasing, inspiring the outside world. Tone—that plus side of your personality that is always vibrating, the radio sending station that broadcasts your personality to all people and insures a welcome reception. Tone—the complexion, the true color of your whole individuality, steady, even, always under control.

All diplomats have tone. It's an essential in your diplomatic makeup, the prelude to all your diplomatic maneuvers.

8. SECRETS OF A GOOD MIXER

Heartiness is the happy front. The man who's bubbling over with obvious good nature isn't going to be hard to get along with.

He turns a stranger into a friend in a second. He always has a cheerful greeting on tap. He doesn't know how to get tired, cranky, morose, or disgusted. Say what you want, the hearty greeter is one of society's noblest creations. Were there no such type, human nature and human intercourse would be pretty dull indeed.

You develop heartiness by simply *showing your heart*. If you like people, make no bones about it. Step out and mix with them to your heart's content and in no time they'll all be calling you by your first name.

When you speak, speak with a robust voice, full of good humor and friendliness. Don't be shy—be hearty, open, forward.

And smile. A good smile is the soul of diplomacy. The first thing a chorus girl has to learn is how to smile. Though her feet are aching, though her mind is elsewhere, though fear and worry are in her heart, she can't get by unless she goes through her routine smiling. Her smile is her best stock in trade and can never be dispensed with!

When you smile, you tell all—friends and strangers alike—"I feel good in myself and toward you. Let's both feel good together!" The other man *has* to chime in; smiling is a contagious disease!

A good hearty handshake is always in order. And again the rule to the right kind of handshake is to put your heart into it. How seldom do you really get a HEARTY HANDSHAKE, a clasping of the other's heart instead of his hand, and the feeling that this is no mere gesture or formality, but an intimate, beautiful, and tender meeting!

Some men greet you with the vise-like grip of a blacksmith. This is more than disgusting, it's revolting. Others just lay a limp cold slab of fish into your hand. The feeling here is like going to step downstairs and missing the steps. But a warm, hearty handshake with just the right pressure—it's an art, a feat, and a memory to cherish. Train yourself to shake hands in this way—put your heart into it!

If you're going to sell yourself through heartiness—be sure your heartiness is natural, simple, buoyant. Then it will be universally pleasing. No one is taken in by false good humor. But everyone falls for a genuine, sincere greeting, robust and sustained good fellowship, and a lot of heart generously exposed at all times.

LET PEOPLE KNOW YOU'RE GLAD TO SEE THEM

You know how you felt the last time you called on that man with whom you had only a slight acquaintance. You were uncertain how he would greet you—if the meeting would be strained, cold, and futile, if, in fact, he would condescend to meet you at all. But when you came into his presence you found him bubbling over with smiles, his welcome was warm and genuine, and he called attention to several incidents of your former contacts which told you that he remembered and cared.

He is the kind of guy you call "regular."

If you'll give people that same impression that you're glad to see them, you'll be called a regular guy, too. The way to give the impression of being glad is actually TO BE GLAD. Enjoy receiving the stranger, the minor acquaintance, the time consuming business associate. Get some fun out of it. Don't dwell mentally on how he's wasting your time! See how many personal good things you can remember with which to cheer him up and make him feel at ease.

The very game of thinking of those cheerful things will make you enjoy the game itself. And so, undoubtedly, you'll give the man the valuable impression that you were glad to see him, an investment that will prove of untold value to you as time goes by.

4. MARKS OF A GOOD YES-MAN

"My idea of an agreeable man," said Samuel Johnson, "is a man who agrees with me."

A yes-man is what everyone is looking for. A man *should* desire contradiction, argument, opposition, in order to whet his brain and keep his mental powers in trim. But hardly anyone is looking for a mental opponent, for a critic, a debater, a rational mind.

We all want the other man to say "Yes." So as long as that is what people are looking for, why not furnish the "Yes" service? The yes-man is always beloved, always popular, always assure of the friendship of his associates. They like the yesing.

A good yes-man isn't just a yes-man in words, he yeses in action, too. What the other man wants to do, is exactly what he wants to do. He never has ideas of his own that may conflict with another's. He never has a program of amusement or pleasure till he is sure it will

134

not conflict with the plans of others. He agrees in everything and he aims to agree!

The agreeable man is, therefore, forever courteous, for courtesy supposes the ability to consider the other man's condition and defer to his desires first.

The agreeable man shows the greatest of *tact,* too, and when he finds he must do something in conflict with the plans of his friends, or if he is a salesman, of his prospects or customers, he defers doing it until the time of conflict has passed. He rubs the fur the right way, he keeps well enough just as it is, he never stirs things up.

The agreeable man never criticizes. Though criticism is one of the highest functions of the intellect, it has no place in diplomacy.

Nobody likes a critic. Even though he is not crossing you at the time, when he's operating behind your back, you're suspicious of his bitter critical ability. But when you meet a man who never criticizes anything, you are sure he will never knock or criticize you when you are away from him.

Be agreeable! It's an essential to getting along with people. The simple way to please people is to have the *sincere desire* to please them. Be agreeable to small, unimportant people as well as to important people. Though you can sell yourself and not be a yes-man, by neglecting this diplomatic quality, you throw an extra burden upon your powers of expression. The perfectly rounded out self-salesman is a good diplomat, an out-and-out "pleaser," a man of tone and tact!

135

5. ARE YOU TOO CHEAP?

Someone you know is dead. The question is: Should you or should you not send flowers? On one side, you hear a voice saying: "You'll go broke throwing your money away like this!" While another voice mildly whispers, "Well, the folks would surely like to get the flowers!"

Welcome the opportunity to give gifts. Don't gloat over the fact that someone you know is dead, but—leaving aside all considerations of sentiment—appreciate the fact that here is an appropriate opportunity to give a present. You agree that a gift always works? Well, then take the opportunity.

Only three things can stop you from giving gifts. First, you don't care. Second, you're too cheap. Third, you haven't the money. The third reason should be the only legitimate one, yet strange to say it is hardly ever the one used. For poor people, people in moderate circumstances, very often are the most generous. The desire to express one's self in a genuine and sincere gift generally uncovers the wherewithal to buy the gift.

The two things that stop you from giving are: 1. You don't care. 2. You're too cheap!

Care! If you don't care about your friends and acquaintances in their hour of distress, in their moment of glory or special celebration, then for goodness' sake, at least care enough about yourself and your own future to realize that a well placed present at this time will help put you in solid, will never be forgotten, and will be better than any of a hundred financial investments you can possibly make in the outside world.

Don't be cheap! No one ever went broke giving a present to another at the right time. To smart men everywhere Christmas is nothing very unusual for they make a habit of giving presents constantly and consistently all through the year. They do it voluntarily, yes, gladly, knowing well that the opportunity to give appropriately is worth much more to them than the price of the present.

You can check whether or not you're cheap by examining your own thoughts. If, every time you see a chance to give an appropriate present, you immediately begin contemplating the cost and proving to yourself that the cost is hardly justified, you can know for sure that you are cheap.

Don't be cheap! Loosen up, take a chance with your money. If, however, you cannot suffer the pangs of your torn purse, act anyhow, give the present in spite of the fact that it goes against the grain. Give because it is practical, if not natural!

Welcome the opportunity to give gifts. Take the attitude of constantly seeking the gift-giving opportunity instead of the attitude of blinding yourself to the situation when it arises.

6. LEGITIMATE BRIBERY

Where does bribery cease to be legitimate and become illegitimate? Who knows?

137

More sales in the business world today are made by, and on account of, bribery than through any other single means.

Show me the man who has gone anywhere in business, who is not a first-class briber, and therefore an excellent diplomat!

They all practice it, and so it must be legitimate in one form or another. Its morality may be challenged but its practicality never can!

Those who object to bribery in business are those who don't practice it. They refuse to practice it, not on moral grounds, but simply because they are too *cheap*.

To bribe another, you must give him something. That requires a sacrifice of selfishness. That requires the forfeiture of a present possession as a trade for a future benefit. In other words, bribery requires *vision*.

But it works. Bribery is merely *giving*. If you'll give, you'll sell—it HAS to be, it can't fail!

Here are some of the accepted forms of bribery:

Money. The millionaire who gives his fortune away to the poor is a briber. He bribes his beneficiaries into loving him. A dime given to a beggar is a bribe—a definite means of preventing the bad feeling you would experience by not giving it.

Merchandise. Merchandise is the same as money, from the standpoint of its value, because it costs money. Often it makes a far better impression, not being so crude a gift, and often expressing good taste and judgment that the receiver might not have been able to purchase himself.

138

Now there's hardly any substitute for the gifts that cost you money. If you paid money for the gift, the receiver knows your sentiment is sincere, for the first, and only real test of sincerity is money laid on the line.

But there are spiritual gifts that are as effective as money, and they cost you no money; but in the very act of giving them, your store of these self-same gifts is increased, never diminished. They never fail to work, never fail to sell you and your proposition, but the only fly in the ointment is they are just as hard to part with as real money.

Here they are:

The Gift of Praise—appropriate mention right before the face of the other man of superior qualities he possesses or of deeds he has done well.

The Gift of Service—Doing things for him, especially things having no direct or indirect connection with what you are selling or promoting.

The Gift of Attention—When he talks or acts, listen to him with your whole heart, your whole soul, your whole mind.

The Gift of Inspiration—Planting the seeds of courage and action in his heart, goading him on to greater deeds.

The Gift of Concession—Humbly saying at just the right point, "You're right, I'm wrong!"

The Gift of Consideration—Putting yourself in his shoes, and thus proving your practical understanding of his side of the case; taking care of the mechanics of human action.

The Gift of Gratitude—Never forgetting to say "thank you" and never failing to mean it.

The Gift of Your Physical Presence—In sickness, trouble, or the hour of glory, going with your body into his presence, so he actually knows your sympathy or congratulations are REAL; not just "being with him in spirit" BECAUSE HE IS NO MIND READER!

How could anyone use these gifts—use any one or more of them and fail to be a good diplomat? How can ANY GIVER EVER FAIL TO SELL HIMSELF!

Don't just acknowledge the practicality of the gift—use it. Drive all the cheapness out of your system—open up—GIVE!

7. PAY YOUR DEBT BEFORE IT'S DUE

When another has earned a reward that you in honor must pay him, don't wait to pay him "eventually"; pay him ahead of the due date. You've got to pay it anyhow, and if you wait till it's due, it becomes a straight payment and not a gift at all. *Make a gift* out of the obligation by paying it ahead of time. This stamps you as strong, generous, appreciative, and adroitly wins for you a return obligation from the person receiving your bounty.

8. GO OUT OF YOUR WAY TO BE NICE

To be nice to people is to be polite. Politeness pays.

But there are two kinds of politeness, the passive kind and the active kind. Passive politeness consists in being nice when people approach you. Fine! Be that way!

But the bigger idea of politeness is the ACTIVE kind. Go out of your way to be nice to people. Anticipate their situation by considering things from their point of view. Then carry politeness to them, without waiting for them to come half way. Grant their requests before they ask them. Offer them those little comforts and conveniences all people appreciate. Take account of their strangeness and help them feel at home quickly. Go out of your way to be nice, and you secure the lifelong allegiance of those you befriend, their boosting, their gratitude and influence.

9. LEFT-HANDED COMPLIMENTS ARE ALWAYS GOOD

There's a way to be apparently disagreeable and at the same time be supremely pleasing. Tactics such as the following are often necessary to reduce the obvious volume of honey and give your diplomacy a change of pace.

Criticize the other person on his strength! For instance, to say to another: "You're too stubborn, too darn bull-headed!" is apparently a criticism, and negative. Actually it is a high compliment for you have insisted that the only fault you find with him is that he isn't weak.

Again, "You're always right, darn it, why can't you be wrong once in a while?" is a very delightful way to be a master diplomat without being an obvious yes-man.

141

Criticize the other on his strength. Ascertain what his strongest quality is, and then, blame the man for possessing the grand virtue to such a high degree: Don't find any fault with the quality itself. Tell him he's too smart, too clever, too strong, too logical. That's criticism —*diplomatic* criticism!

10. LEAVE A GOOD TASTE IN THEIR MOUTHS

A tasty dessert has often redeemed an otherwise disappointing meal. Whatever you do, be sure to make a good finish. Speed, class and dash, shown in the wind-up, often serve to obscure poorer work in the middle stages. By all means save the best of you for the finish. Whether it be a public performance, a private sale, an individual job, be sure to bring it to the very best possible conclusion.

11. AVOID THE OPEN BREAK

When another has displeased or hurt you, an overwhelming temptation prompts you to go and tell him to his face. What do you gain? If, when he hurt your feelings, he was clearly in the wrong, he doubtless knew it, and your telling him can't have an object or good. Rather, your wrath may start an open brawl or a bitter rift in your friendship or acquaintance. But why show him how mad you are? YOU HAVE NOTHING TO GAIN! On the other hand, you have much to gain by preserving silence, by letting the matter pass; for tomorrow your normal activities may require an association with the man, and if you make an enemy out of him today, you can't associate with him tomorrow under any circumstances. Invest in the future—avoid the open break!

Invisible Diplomacy

All your diplomacy must have a hidden objective, the end you are seeking. This objective is absolutely clear to you, but thoroughly obscured from the notice of others. You must never let your mind wander away from the object of your diplomacy. You must silently mention this objective to yourself, over and over, and you proceed to pull the strings that may cause the happy result.

If you keep your objective constantly before you, you quickly develop the keenness that allows you to distinguish instantly between the things that are useful and the things that aren't. You seize your useful means as quickly as they present themselves; you reject the useless items without hesitation.

The amateur diplomat is always sorely tempted to tell the world about what he is doing. So inexperienced is he that he wants to let everyone see his diplomacy in action, wants to publish his own cleverness in bringing about the predicted result even before it does happen. He often even goes so far as to inform the victims of diplomacy about all these matters and thus makes it impossible for his diplomacy to work at all. The penalty of amateurism!

143

Tell them nothing! Keep your own counsel. Never let anybody know what you are trying to do. NEVER PUT ALL YOUR CARDS ON THE TABLE. Keep your eye on your own private goal eternally and then you will never be at a loss to act effectively when the right opportunity presents itself.

That goal—if it is legitimate—belongs to you. The means of reaching that goal—if legitimate—also belong to you. There is no duty of sportsmanship or morality that requires that you tell people what you are doing. If you have such a communicative streak you'll never get anywhere with it. The silence of the true diplomat is profound.

1. DON'T SAY WHAT YOU THINK!

It is seldom expedient to mention out loud everything you think.

If you have an uncontrollable urge to speak the truth, in spite of all costs, see if you can't quash this urge by better understanding your position and that of your listeners.

First of all, though you pride yourself on your great openness and honesty, your right and your inclination to always say what you think, YOU DON'T ACTUALLY SAY WHAT YOU THINK RIGHT NOW. As a matter of fact you stifle your urge to speak the truth about ninety per cent of the time.

If, for instance, you meet a cripple or a person with a pronounced physical deformity, you have enough good breeding and enough politeness not to comment on their condition.

"Truth," you have declared, "is uppermost! Nothing can supersede it!" That is not so at all. In the above case politeness supersedes truth—and politeness is just one form of expediency.

It is no less worthy to refrain from saying what you think in behalf of some other form of expediency.

Your principal inclination to say what you think runs along the lines of criticism, contradiction, argument, prejudice, and pointed observation.

Actually you say what you think about ten per cent of the time and this saying of what you think is done not out of any grand duty or blind worship of the truth but principally for the effect you hope to create by taking the opposite side. Truth isn't so necessary for you that you will always speak it. So when you say what you think, you must admit that you say it principally for effect.

Now just what is the effect? Discord, discouragement, friction, bitterness, and UNPOPULARITY! No one admires, respects, or LIKES you for having said what you think. In rejoinder, you say you don't care. But you do—for your principal urge to speak out was to show everybody how smart and individualistic you were and thereby gain an effect.

But the effect is all left-handed! It gets you nothing. It leaves you in a poor light. And instead of feeling better within yourself for having been true to your convictions you actually feel worse.

Don't say what you think! (That's not lying. Lying is saying what you don't think!) Go after an effect, yes, but let that be the effect of pleasing your audience, of stroking people's fur the right way, of being a warm, sociable, easy-to-get-on-with sort of fellow. Call it hypocrisy, call it desertion, call it anything you want—*but it can't be wrong!* For never will your conscience be more at ease, never will your heart be more at peace than when you are stifling the urge to say what you think when that something is unfavorable, inappropriate, or injurious. Rather, by stroking people's fur the right way, you get that feeling of spiritual uplift destined for the heavenly few. Nothing that can make you feel so noble and exalted could be wrong!

2. PLAY POLITICS TO A FARE-THEE-WELL

If you work at a job, that job is subject to the influence of surrounding politics.

If you are in business for yourself, politics in a large way dictates your activities.

Most of us make the mistake of submitting to politics, of letting politics take its toll from us, as if it is something that has to be suffered. But that is the wrong principle. *Control your own politics instead of letting politics control you!*

There is very little difference between private politics, the politics surrounding your job, your business, your position in society, and public politics, the political machinations which elect men to public office.

You can't go wrong by taking your political lessons from the machinations of public politicians. Some of these activities are low and reprehensible, too difficult for many a man of character to stomach, and yet they afford the practical material for winning the battles of diplomacy.

Public politics are based strictly on *organization*. A political "machine," to be effective, must be a *machine*. The cogs of the machine are, first, the precinct workers and the precinct captains. Politicians, in serving their own ends, are thorough; they go all the way. They don't want to see that single last vote escape their net. The precinct being the smallest political subdivision, they have at least one worker and often five or six in each precinct. This worker, at election time, personally interviews *every* voter. He makes promises. He uses, where fitting, implied threats. He points to past favors. He gets his votes spoken for before election day ever comes round.

The political rule above him is hard and ruthless. He, the precinct captain, now holds a public job due entirely to the beneficence of the party he serves. IF HE DOESN'T CARRY HIS PRECINCT, however, this job may be taken from him. So he turns in a superhuman amount of work to carry the majority of votes in his precinct. The general public often scoffs at this doorbell pusher, wonders where he gets off, mildly despises his quality and character, and considers him the lightest of lightweights. *Yet he is the man who wins elections. He* is the *organization!*

Above him are the sectional bosses, who control wards, senatorial and congressional districts, but they don't really control wards, they control precinct captains. The better their control, the stronger the power.

Organization tells them where every vote is, the leverage that can be applied in each individual case, and the machine generally wins through its detailed thoroughness and the applied energies of its workers.

The fuel that makes the machine go is of three kinds: Favors, threats, and promises. Jobs are given out. The jobs will be taken away if the jobholder fails to do his part. But if success attends his efforts, an even richer plum may be waiting for him.

8. YOUR PRIVATE BRAND SHOULD COPY THE "BIG TIME" VARIETY

In working your private politics, you can't miss if you copy the pattern of this public political machine. First of all, you must have something to give: Favors, promises of profits or promotions. Place these favors judiciously, where you know the receivers will acknowledge their dependence on you. Out of these favors and using these individuals you perfect your organization. You know what each man can deliver. You see to it that he DOES deliver.

That's the view from the top! From the bottom, there's a much less colorful view for the insignificant individual who is working his way up.

The little man, trying to enter politics from the bottom, has first to "snoop around." It is necessary that he have a news nose that tells him who is the man that can aid him in getting this first job, then he soft-soaps him, toadies to him, becomes his messenger boy, his man Friday. He must not only be this kind of knee bender, he must also be persevering. He must continue in his ministrations until he gets the job or favor he is seeking and then keep right on the same track with even greater fervor. This is the basic law of politics. No one has ever succeeded in cheating it a single iota. The big boss, before whom all the other politicians now bow down, in his young years kowtowed completely to the man above him.

In politics it is just as bad as that—and worse! In business it isn't quite so bad because individual talent has more merit accruing to it there. But for people in miscellaneous, not special, work, it is all important that they submit intelligently to the political rule above them, that they flatter, conciliate, and humbly serve the one above who can promote them.

And then observe the common understanding traditionally existing between the political favor-giver and favor-receiver. No double-crossing! No going over the head of the higher-up! It never works. You are always found out, and because that other man is stronger than you, you cannot defeat him in the uneven contest.

In your sphere of work you have your choice of either playing politics or not. If you don't play politics you may be left out of the swim. If you do play politics, never be so foolish as to try to set up any new or different rules—YOU HAVE TO PLAY THE SAME GAME all politicians have played since the world began!

Rather than being a victim of politics, you should pay considerable attention to the conditions under which you work, cultivate the favor of the man above who can most help you, organize the support of those under you who have received your favors, pay full attention to all details and incidentals, and never be satisfied till the votes are in and the election is won!

4. NOTHING IS SACRED IN POLITICS—EXCEPT GRATITUDE

Here is the only sacred rule of politics: *Be grateful.*

Of course the chief criticism commonly hurled against politicians is the cry of "ingratitude!" Most politicians are poor politicians. It's true they're ingrates. That's why they're condemned by both insiders and outsiders and never get very far in the game.

But the politician who gets to the top never forgets his faithful supporters, never refuses to acknowledge a favor received. His unfailing rule for passing out the plums is: Who are the *deserving* ones?

The beauty of gratitude isn't that it is noble, but that it is practical. If you remember and are grateful to those who remembered you in the past, you will acquire the reputation of being a grateful man. Though some will claim rewards who have never earned those rewards, and will envy you the favors you do for those who have earned the rewards, they will at least acknowledge that you are "paying back."

150

Become known as a man who "pays back" and you automatically invite hundreds of others to do favors for you today knowing full well that their future rewards are guaranteed. There is no more practical a department of politics than gratitude. Whether you love the man or despise him, be grateful *if he has it coming!*

5. LOSING GROUND TO GAIN GROUND

Often in driving through heavy city traffic the experienced motorist deliberately goes blocks, sometimes miles, out of his way in order to avoid congestion. He doubles his tracks, adds extra distance to his journey, loses ground. But he does this deliberately because he actually gets to his destination faster than if he took the shortest and most direct route.

In playing politics you have to lose ground to gain ground. You never have the field entirely to yourself. You must take account of opposition, you must overcome obstacles—seldom by fighting them or ploughing straight through them but by conceding, sacrificing, compromising.

The trained politician avoids all harshness, bitterness, savagery. They call him "oily" because he believes in reducing friction to the absolute minimum.

In avoiding friction by conceding or compromising, be sure to make the necessary distinction between the different kinds of concessions.

There's the *unimportant* concession. This costs you nothing at all, perhaps with just a little scratch to your pride. Never insist on holding to your side when analysis shows there is nothing at all at stake. Concede and save time!

There's the *important* concession. This costs you something tangible, in money, power, or advancement. Regard the making of such a concession in the light of a real investment. If the benefits are worth the costs, make it. If it doesn't look like a good investment, don't make it.

There's the concession *which hasn't been earned by the party demanding it.* Always analyze the proposed or contemplated concession to see if it is justified. Perhaps you are only being bluffed, and you can't be hurt by your refusal to concede. Maybe the other party is trying to get something for nothing. Don't give it.

6. "LEAVE HIM WITH A SMILE": A HINT TO EMPLOYEES AND EMPLOYERS

On leaving any job for a better one, you have a great temptation to tell your old employer what you think of him and his methods.

Don't do it! Leave him with a smile!

You'll never know at what time in the future you will need his good-will, his help. Leave him with a smile now! To retain that relationship is the most important thing you can do on departing from your old connection. Who knows but that in a year or two you may want to come back to the old place? Or who knows but that where you may be working in the future you may be required to seek business from the old concern?

Retain your employer's good-will even after you have left him. Make it your business to see him once in a while, to write to him, to send him Christmas cards, to remember him on special occasions. That friendship is invaluable from the standpoint of business. From the standpoint of pure character, of sociability, and *loyalty* it is still more important. *Be loyal to the firm even after you leave it.*

Always speak good of your old employer and your old firm. To speak of *them* in bitter terms is merely to condemn yourself, to have people judge you meanly. To boost them is to boost yourself.

And, Mr. Employer, let your employee leave with a smile. If you dismiss him, do it as gracefully as possible, be fair and honest about the explanation you give him. If he leaves voluntarily, don't be mad about it, congratulate him and wish him well. You never know when that former employee may be in a position controlling a great deal of business you seek. If he is mad at you, you are out! If you still have his favor and respect, you are in!

Leave him with a smile!

153

☆

_____

Familiarity

The word Familiarity comes from the Latin *familia*. It means *family*.

Familiarity is the ability to put yourself in the other person's family. If you can do that, he will treat you as a brother. He will feel safe in dealing with you. You will *belong* in his class.

The personal quality of familiarity must absolutely be established before the other person hires you, accepts you, takes you up with the idea of boosting you to his friends. His support cannot be won unless you are of his same psychological blood.

People don't marry one another till each has established trust through familiarity. So deep rooted is the necessity for this familiarity that often there appears an astonishing physical resemblance between husband and wife. The man subsconsciously picks out the kind of girl who looks like his mother and sisters and the girl picks out the kind of man who looks like her father and brothers.

Actually each picks out the kind of person who LOOKS like himself or herself! And there is nothing so unusual about it for when you examine just a few cases of where people have sold themselves to others, you often find this same amazing physical resemblance ruling the stage and dictating the decisions.

Now it isn't necessary that you *look like* the man in order to stand in with him. In general there are three basic types of familiarity and all of them are effective. In hardly any case can you use all of them to help you achieve your objective. You don't need to. Just one or two of the methods will do the trick. You are given a wide choice of methods simply because it will be your duty to meet and sell a wide variety of people. What works on the first man won't work on the second and what works on the second may not take with the second hundredth! But just see how many ways there are to enter the psychological family of anybody on earth!

1. WHAT KIND OF BUDDY ARE YOU?

Any two people are members of one or more groups or families. For instance, there's a man whose favor you seek. He went to the same school you did. He went a long time before you did. It wasn't a high school or college, it was only grammar school. Now that's a very faint and distant connection—yet actually it is a definite connection, even though extremely minor. And it may even be used to effect the meeting you desire.

But supposing the man wasn't merely an alumnus of your grammar school. Suppose he was an alumnus of the university from which you graduated. Suppose that instead of being a member of a former class, he was an actual *classmate;* for four intense and thrilling years you went through college work and college play together. Even though you haven't seen, heard from or corresponded with the man for thirty years, you even now KNOW that you can approach him with PERFECT SAFETY and be confident that if favors are to be given you have a good chance at the inside track.

A very large percentage of all commercial selling uses the great advantages that accrue to members of the same families. The person you are selling doesn't have to be related to you by blood or marriage.

He may be a member of the same lodge.

Of the same nationality. How silly a thing to suppose that that should matter—but it does!

Of the same neighborhood. You both get on the train at the same station. Yes, that's something! And if the man's your next door neighbor, that's a great deal more.

The same social circle. You entertain, visit, drink beer, play golf, root for the same ball team, as the other fellow. It's a big advantage.

Of the same church. That often becomes a real holy bond! Sometimes it is a matter of bigotry, but a good opportunist collects his favors in whatever way he can!

Of the same *anything*. *Same* is the magic word in familiarity of membership. A little study will disclose how you and the other are actual members of the same actual group. Then all you have to do is stress this fellowship that is implied in the membership.

2. MAKE YOUR HOBBIES PAY DIVIDENDS

Mental familiarity is achieved by having the:

Same ideals. If both you and the other person cherish and extol the same things, a common inspiration will draw you instantly together. Few bonds are stronger than the familiarity that grows out of having the same ideals. Ideals raise you high above the smallness and cheapness of other familiarity, they draw forth greater support, greater favor simply because nothing in them involves small trading or exchange.

If you are seeking favor, you certainly should be seeking it from big people. Big people have ideals. So you should be sure to have some of your own. Develop these ideals first, then never hesitate to break out with them in the presence of the big people. Because, even if the other person hasn't the same ideals as you, if he is idealistic on his own part, he will recognize and respond to the strain in you. And in a short while you both will be having the same ideals!

Same likes. If you're a good golf player and he's a good golf player, pretty soon you and he will be getting together.

Nothing can stop that simple formula. It has been

worked a million times and it will be worked many million times more. By being bugs about the same game, by being competent in the same activity, you are drawn together, even closer than many blood brothers.

So common is this principle that it cannot even be overworked! The clever salesman always pretends a consuming interest in the buyer's hobbies, just to stand in his good graces. Very often he is neutral; even dislikes the thing the buyer raves about. But he joins him just the same, even though sometimes he is insincere.

How much better it is to join with the man sincerely —by the simple means of honestly discovering what it is YOU BOTH LIKE. When it's one-sided familiarity, when only he likes the thing truly and you merely pretend to like it, somehow or other deep down the man knows of your discrepancy. Because he is so enthusiastic on the subject, he welcomes *any* kind of co-responsiveness from you, but if your co-responsiveness is *genuine,* then it reaches its highest degree of effect.

And it's simply a matter of probing till you find the thing or things on which you both are in perfect accord. *Have you the same tastes*—be it only such a mild thing as your both liking black coffee, or colonial architecture, fishing, handball, walking, or the same magazine! If you are driving and meet another car of the same *make* as yours, you feel an instant familiarity for the owner of that car, just because he likes and selects the same thing you liked and selected. It's a far-fetched expression of familiarity of taste, yet a very effective one. How strong, therefore, is the link when you meet the man

159

face to face and are able to discuss personally the several considerations that prove you think alike, feel alike
and act alike! You like the same things. You have the
same dispositions, inclinations, and habits. You are alike
—and therefore you like each other, and feel forever
safe in dealing with each other!

3. BE YOURSELF

There can never be any excuse for your failure to produce *sentimental or emotional familiarity.*

There's a reason why people say they dislike others.

There's a reason why people are afraid of others.

There's a reason why people aren't interested in
others.

All of these reasons center around the simple fact
that they don't *know* the others. And they don't know
them simply because others have failed to *show themselves.*

Oscar Wilde once remarked satirically: "Man's first
duty in life is to be as artificial as possible!" And the
world, unconsciously, goes about fulfilling that false
duty every day of the year. So we find practically ALL
people forced—artificial—strained—affected—saying
and acting things that in no way express their true
nature, pretending to be characters and personalities
entirely foreign to their true characters and personalities.

That's why the person who is able enough and wise
enough to drop all artificiality and be *his true self* has

such a chance to win instant popularity. He simply establishes sentimental familiarity by *being himself*.

The first way to achieve this rich familiarity is to *drop all shame*. Every human heart is the reservoir of millions of private experiences and emotions which it thinks it alone of all the hearts in the world is carrying. For some reason—which it would take a psychiatrist to explain—the heart, and the person possessing it, is quietly but drastically *ashamed* of these emotions and experiences.

What a relief it is, when one finds another living person who in an unguarded moment shows a side of himself which clearly proves he has the same intimate emotions as you thought only you possessed! You warm to him at once, you feel that he alone can understand you, that the two of you belong together forever.

But if you take a broad view of your own emotions you suddenly learn that every adult on the face of the globe has had practically all the same thoughts, feelings, and intimate shames that you have had! We laugh at children because they do things we would do if we weren't *ashamed* to do them! We laugh, too, when the grown-up clown or comedian exposes thoroughly adult feelings that were thought our own private property. We laugh singly and we laugh as a crowd, and yet we never stop to think that crowd of a thousand people, now laughing with us, is individually and collectively the victim of this same private shame as we.

The cue is *be yourself!* Shed shame, say and do what you really think and feel. People won't think you peculiar, they will love you because you really are yourself!

Sentimental familiarity originates in the shedding of shame, but there are several definite exemplifications of this principle which help you achieve familiarity at will. Here are some of them:

Familiar patter. There are tens of thousands of expressions, sometimes called slang, sometimes called bromides or chestnuts, which are the common property of all people. Phrases like "Pretty as a picture," "So help me Jake!" "Don't know him from Adam," "Pain in the neck," "Stop, look, and listen," "Ye gods!" "Laugh that off!" "Move heaven and earth," "Taking candy from a baby," "Getting out the wrong side of the bed," etc., get the real ideas across!

The phrases have been used over and over a million times. They are popular because they have in them the elements which guarantee a clean-cut transmission of meaning.

After all, the purpose of language is to convey meaning. Familiar language makes the meaning clear and you more familiar and better understood!

Actions speak louder. If you want your children to say their prayers, don't you merely *tell* them to say their prayers. They do what you do, not what you say. So you say your own, and pretty soon, they may be peeking around a door and find you on your knees praying, and the force of this one genuine example will be as powerful as a thousand thundering commands or threats!

Repeat till they're groggy. People's memories are proverbially weak. Say anything once, and they immediately forget it. Say it ten times, and it makes a short-lived impression. But say it a hundred times and more and then they finally realize what you mean. It takes repetition, unrelenting, untiring, unvarying repetition to get your ideas over. But if you succeeded in getting them to remember only ONE thing about you, you have definitely established your familiarity with them for life.

One, two, three. simplicity. Don't ask too much of people's understanding. Keep your message short. Keep its points in order. One, two, three. Take the professional attitude and deliberately waste a great deal of the information you have by *not* using it! Use simple words, short sentences, unembellished experience. Talk of things that everybody knows, such as fire escape, baked apple, snowball, dish rag, street car. People will like you if they can only *understand* you. Preserve simplicity and you build familiarity!

'Fess up. An honest confession of your mistakes, your private feelings, your silly and distorted thoughts, often does much to draw another to you because nearly always your mistakes and shortcomings are his own.

Translate your meaning. Just because you say the words in English, it doesn't mean others will understand you. Avoid unusual words, abstract ideas, scientific or technical expressions. That man is most professional who speaks or writes so that all people, whether professionals or not, can understand him instantly.

1. Put your meaning in a story or anecdote. The

parables in the Bible were an effective way of teaching moral principles.

2. Simile ("Like a duck takes to water") or metaphor ("A mountain of a man") are standard devices for getting people to understand, or at least to *feel* they understand.

3. Find and express the human interest. Ideas, such as baby, mother, sweetheart, Christmas, are connected with the deepest sentiments of the the human heart. Uncover the human interest and people will warm to you at once!

4. Humor. If you are funny, don't try to conceal it. The world wants to laugh and will love you for giving it the opportunity. If you are not funny, don't try to be funny.

5. Bring in the old-fashioned! If you have modern ideas, use them, but don't parade them. People are afraid of what is new and untried. In the realm of ideas, especially, they love the old-fashioned, they love to recall and to reminisce.

    They are not afraid of something which they have all experienced and which they still easily remember.

6. Quotation. You know how, when reading a book of fiction, your eye often is tempted to skip the

164

intermediate sections and take the dialog only. Those quotation marks around the dialog are irresistible. So also, can you bring acceptance and understanding to your own remarks, if you adroitly use quotations from famous men in history or prominent people of today. Page Mr. Shakespeare, Napoleon, Alexander, Cleopatra, King Solomon and the rest! If a famous man said it, it ought to be easy to understand!

4. CULTIVATE THE UNIVERSAL STREAK

You can nicely substitute for not having the same hobby as the other man, by developing in yourself THE UNIVERSAL STREAK.

The universal streak is the ability to respond to anything, an object, a person, or an activity, through an instantaneous and natural attempt to *understand* it. If you will but practice at bending your mind to react instantly to ALL things and ALL people you will not be long in developing the universal streak.

You must be alert to all things.

You must be everlastingly interested in all things and in every new thing the instant it comes up.

Your mind must be harnessed by no prejudices, no confining activities of its own. *You must be broadminded.*

"Broadminded" is simply the state of removing all restrictions to your mind's normal and natural operations.

Broadminded people are universally familiar because of their universal streak. The world likes to deal with the man it knows, the man it likes, the man it feels safe with, the FAMILIAR MAN.

Be broadminded and you'll automatically possess an abundance of familiarity with all people.

5. BE SYMPATHETIC!

If you're looking for sympathy, the wag will tell you to try Webster or Funk & Wagnalls on page so-and-so.

But a joke about sympathy is no joke at all.

If there's one thing the whole world is looking for it is sympathy.

As you go about selling yourself, be sure your stock of sympathy is kept up to par at all times. Be ready to supply it in lavish volume at a moment's notice.

Sympathy means "feeling with" and it's not difficult to "feel with" the other person, if you will master the trick of forgetting all about yourself at will.

Forget yourself, consider that man in front of you. He, like you, is full of sentiment, emotion, fears, desires, strength and weakness. But it's his favor that you're seeking, he's not trying to get a stand-in with you, but he can certainly use some of your sympathy (he gets none whatever from his wife, his children, his brothers and sisters, his business associates). Stifle your own feelings and turn on the sympathy.

Think and feel with that man in HIS situation. If he has just suffered defeat, just been through the excruci-

166

ating toils of misery, let it be your defeat, your misery, and suffer with him. What's hard about that? You can do it and do it genuinely and sincerely—if you will only forget your selfishness.

Sympathy is the great unlisted beatitude. All it needs is a consciousness of another's condition and a complete unconsciousness of one's own. Its practical reward is the favor and friendship of the person to whom the sympathy is extended, but a richer, fuller reward is the grand journey into another's life, the glorious escape from your own selfishness, the thrill of enduring another's grief, another's setbacks, another's heart pumping another's blood right through your own veins! A higher, purer, more humane act than the thousand of dull matter-of-fact things you do in an ordinary lifetime.

Sympathy doesn't necessarily mean grief or sorrow. Remember it means "feeling with." If that other man has just tasted the ecstasy of victory, taste it with him. Recount for 'him the delicious steps that made his triumph possible, so that he can go over his victory again and again, feeling a happiness in communing with you that he could never experience alone.

Out of such sympathy comes the bond of familiarity. You become more than a friend, more than a brother, you become the man's other self. You are united with him forever and your STAND-IN IS DEFINITELY ESTABLISHED. Sympathy is a gilt-edged investment. You have an unlimited fund and it costs you nothing to dispense it to a hungry populace. Be sympathetic!

167

6. "HIGH-KEYED" GENERALLY MEANS "HIGH-SALARIED"

A high-keyed person is one who is able to "catch on" very quickly and very easily. He is the person who can tune in on any new subject, however strange or abstruse, and vibrate to it in perfect time without any previous training whatsoever.

A high-keyed man hasn't necessarily a superior intelligence; though he is most often smart in the real meaning of the word, he can be high-keyed and yet not overly smart.

To the high-keyed man, the world and the people in it are an open book, and a book that belongs to him. For he cannot go anywhere without being instantly at home. He cannot run into anything that must be endured for more than a few minutes without understanding it and being close to it. Such a man may have been in a certain line of business for several years, yet tomorrow step into an altogether different line of business and know the new business better in a few weeks than another person who had been in it all his life.

Yet the high-keyed man is not a genius, necessarily, and not necessarily smart! He's just high-keyed. He has a gift for ignoring surface qualities and responding to basic natures. He gets at the heart of the thing before he even notices the clothes or the voice.

To be high-keyed is one of the richest possessions of human nature. You are never lost. You are never scared by new or unknown things or people. You have a grasp on life even greater than the philospher in all his wisdom. *For you are always in tune, wherever you go!*

Being high-keyed you sell yourself by assimilating the other's character and personality instantly and sharing similar emotions and understanding. If he has a product, a subject, a situation that is his peculiarity, the chances are he has met few people who understand it in the way he does. But as soon as he meets you, he is immediately amazed and delighted. You know the thing, you feel the thing, EXACTLY the way he does!

Key yourself high—yes, high, wide, and handsome! Ready to tune in to any new person, any new thing, any question or situation, without preparation or training, without fear or awkwardness. You can do it—you can acquire this astonishing faculty which causes other people to grasp you and hold you as a prized possession.

The way to a high-keyed personality is through a simple rule: *Pay Attention!* PAY ATTENTION! Instead of worrying: "Am I going to make a dunce of myself by not understanding it? How can that fellow expect me to know as much about his pet subject as he does? Where in my past have I met anything like this?"

You throw every single thought and emotion out of your system, you forfeit every bit of previous knowledge and experience you may have on the subject, and face the new situation strictly *as a new situation.*

You are about to learn something new—*quickly!* If it's new, you want no connection with your own past, no previous knowledge to help you. You're going to learn it ALL—right now!

So pay attention—and with this distinction: Pay

169

attention not too definitely with your *mind,* but COM-PLETELY and PERFECTLY with your SENSES.

The mind takes time to formularize, to deduce, to get new knowledge in shape to retain and master.

The senses work instantly!

If you would be high-keyed, pay attention with your senses! Hear the thing, taste it, touch it, feel it, smell it, talk it with your external senses. And with your internal senses *drift* into it with your instinct; fabricate it with your imagination; photograph it with your memory; organize it with your common sense. The five external and the four internal senses are your high-keyed machine which is ever ready to race with immense speed, perform herculean tasks, travel far or wide to do anything new or unusual.

A clumsily working mind, an inferiority attitude of the intellect very often work havoc with the senses, paralyzing them temporarily and blocking all new knowledge from entering.

But for a high-keyed personality, separate your mind from your senses, keep them free, pay intense attention with them and them only. There's plenty of time for your mind later to get formal and scientific; your present task is to get this new thing informally, but truly; *get its real nature!*

The senses working without restriction give you a miraculous new flow of life for the new subject; you live the thing from babyhood to maturity in a few moments. Wherever you go, you respond to your fellow man and your fellow man responds to you.

170

7. CALL HIM BY HIS FIRST NAME

Few artifices help to consolidate familiarity more than the simple stunt of calling another by his first name.

The general belief is that it's presumption, and a mistake, to call a stranger or a brand-new acquaintance by his first name. That is not always so. You may just meet a friend of your brother, a man whom you have heard much of, but never saw before in your life. It would be a mistake to call him "Mister." His familiarity with one close to you demands equal familiarity from you.

The word "Mister" is often a big hurdle. You just know it is the wrong word to use, because the man to whom you give the formal title may be shocked, astonished, or hurt by its formality. You then have to make a choice between using his last name—which manner of address is cold, stiff, and distant, sometimes even insulting—or his first name.

When in doubt, use the first name! How many times have you been offended by people, people only remotely connected with you, calling you by your first name? Not very often! Yet many times have you been made to feel rather queer because others called you mister, hailed you brutally by your last name, or deliberately avoided giving you any salutation at all. The first name is generally a compliment; it shows the desire to be friendly; it sounds young, buoyant, happy; it expresses a willingness to share the situation equally.

But calling another by his first name doesn't *of it-*

self create acceptable familiarity. The first name simply expresses an established *state* or *relationship*. Your big object is to achieve a definite relationship with the other which is unquestionably a "first name" relationship. This will spring from your own willingness to be a friend to him. A fine way to practice getting yourself into this disposition is to *think of him always by his first name.* That is, when you are mentally considering the man and his activities, call him "Dave," or "John," or "Harry," and not Miller, Smith, or Jones, as the case may be. In no time at all, if you use the first name mentally, you will have established your right to use it orally.

Just as a first name creates a bond of friendship and familiarity, so also the use of a good nickname produces the same effect. Never use the nickname if it is sissified or ridiculous. Names like "Bull," "Big," "Speed" are complimentary and effective. Names like "Mush-mouth," "Nuts" are ridiculous and should be avoided. Never be so foolhardy as to tack a brand new nickname on a man. He may curse you for life!

In the same way avoid calling a man by his correct Christian name if it is in any way fancy. You just know "Vincent," "Francis," "Cecil" will not go over. Shorten them into "Vince," "Frank," and "Cece." Sometimes a person has an intense dislike for a certain name or nick-name. It is always well to check with the person, openly and sincerely, to make sure you are not touching a sore spot every time you use a name which seems all right with you, but which is anathema to him.

8. DOES FAMILIARITY BREED CONTEMPT?

Is there a word of warning in the old phrase that you should harken to as you go about developing your personal quality of familiarity?

No!

In the saying, "Familiarity breeds contempt," the word "familiarity" is synonymous with "intimacy." In developing sentimental or emotional familiarity, it is not necessary to achieve personal intimacy nor, in fact, is it wise to do so.

The sole object of familiarity is that people know you and understand you. It is never necessary or advisable that they take you to their bosom.

It is necessary, however, that the familiarity you achieve be definitely *favorable* to you. The man who makes himself into a clown or public fool is familiar, but his familiarity is a handicap for it only breeds contempt.

☆

Reliability

The reliable people are the ones who make the wheels of the world go round. They are the engineers, the mechanics, the straight thinkers, the men who prescribe for the world's ills and bring order out of chaos.

By all the rules of merit, they should be the most important people in the world and the world's laurels should be resting proudly on their brows. But alas, such is not the case! The world's laurels go to the reliable person only when he is something more than reliable, that is, when he is not only able to deliver the goods but in addition is able to *sell himself!*

Reliability is a necessary quality in selling yourself, but in order of importance it is Number Seven on the list. Still, the fact that it is placed behind six other qualities does not mean that it can ever be dispensed with. It is especially useful if your accomplishments in selling yourself are faulty and insufficient; it is superbly useful where it reinforces great expression, or where it deals with inanimate forces and the personal equation is missing.

The chief bases of reliability are *truth* and *ability*. Truth is *what is*. Ability is *the power to do*. When a person is able to know the truth and avoid error, and can operate the truth so as to solve the problem, produce the goods, serve the economic fulfillment of the task, he is *a reliable person*. And there are all too few of them in the world!

In selling yourself it is necessary that you both *have* Reliability and that you also *carry the marks* of reliability, which is a very desirable means of securing recognition for your special skill and prowess. You sell your reliability just like you sell your personality. *Let people see it!*

There are four main divisions of Reliability: Character, Ability, Self-Confidence, Conservativeness.

Character

1. THE ANCHOR OF YOUR PERSONALITY

Character is the anchor of your personality. Without character, all your ability, all your personal gifts, may count for naught.

The quickest way to detect absence of character is by inconsistency, changeableness, vacillation. A man who changes cannot be known, and character is nothing unless it is known. It is in the essence of character that it merits faith, trust, reliance; that it be single in nature; that it be open, visible, knowable; that it be strong and unyielding.

Thus we see that character cannot deceive, cannot change, cannot be two things at the same time.

You can't expect to have a perfect character, but you can, and SHOULD, have enough character to earn you the title of "a man of character." To hold this title, there are certain rules that can never be broken, and the first and most important is:

2. YOU MUST NOT BE "TWO-FACED"

You cannot be all things to all men! You must be the same thing to all men, and you must not be afraid to say to a man's face what you delight in saying behind his back.

We pick for friends those people who have character. They are our friends, and they have character we respect, because we know we can rely on their being the same to us behind our backs as they are to our faces. To be different would not be a friend, but a traitor.

It is not good to talk about people behind their backs, that is to talk unfavorably. If you have to do so, say those things which you are not ashamed or afraid to say to their faces. An honest enemy has ten thousand times as much character as a dishonest "friend."

To observe this one rule, in your relations with others, will do much to develop all the other parts of

177

character you should have. Be consistent! Use your faculties for the purpose for which they are intended. Consistent honesty in dealing with others will make you consistently honest in dealing with yourself. Be consistent! Don't be a pawn in the hands of other players. Don't be a "last man's man," influenced from a new point of view from minute to minute, and having nothing you can cling to permanently. Consistency will teach you to think for yourself, to stand up for your rights, to assume responsibility and to hold to your course.

And there's no better place to start your character building than in your relations with other people. Start today to eliminate every single trace of the "two-faced" taint from your character. Correct this one item, and real nobility of character has every chance to follow.

3. TELL THE TRUTH

A lie never makes any kind of an impression—even if it is believed. If it's an important lie you're found out practically at once, and your transgression is all the more serious. If the lie is not important, what's the use of lying? Tell the truth!

Lying is too great a strain on your memory. You not only have to remember each individual lie, you also have to weave all your lies together in a consistent ensemble, so one won't contradict the other. For the effort required in a perfect job of lying, it would be much better strategy to tell the truth and use your mental gymnastics for some legitimate benefit.

Don't let the epithet "Liar!" be fastened on you. If you are a liar, sooner or later you will be known as a liar—and all chances for building up your reliability will be shattered. The term "Liar!" can never be applied to a truthful man, even unjustly. It just won't stick unless the man is actually a liar.

Tell the truth and act the truth. The essence of truth is consistency. Act consistently. Don't have the things you do one day contradict the things you have done the day previous.

The world is holding a magnifying glass over you, trying to prove you inconsistent. If you act according to the basic principles of truth, they can't catch you in a contradiction. "All true things square."

4. KEEP YOUR PROMISES

Be a man of your word! That's the soundest way to establish your character publicly. If you make a promise, public or private, be sure to do what you promise. If you commit yourself to a program, don't withdraw until you have reached the stated goal.

When you keep your promises you quickly become known as a man who *delivers.* There are so few people in the world *who actually deliver* that the ability to deliver and unimpeachable character are inseparably connected in the eyes of people. The man with character has no alibis or excuses; once engaged in a course of action, all he knows how to do is deliver what he promised, to do the thing THAT HAS TO BE DONE regardless of the circumstances, the obstacles, or the desertions of associates. He delivers, most of the time, delivers single handedly, for the only man anyone can make promises for is himself.

Keep your promises *to yourself* just as faithfully as your promises to others. Be careful about what you do promise yourself; don't promise yourself too many things too often; but when you do make a vow of an agreement that affects only yourself and your own actions, never fail to keep that promise! To break a promise that you make to yourself is the ruination of your own self-respect. Once you cease to believe in your own character, your character begins to disintegrate!

5. BUILD GOOD HEALTH

Somehow or other the man who is in good health carries a genuine air of reliability. There's a glow of life in his eyes, a tint in his cheeks, a firmness and steadiness in his gestures, that just force you to think him reliable.

The three keys to a healthy body are fresh air, good food, and plenty of rest. A well controlled nervous system is also an invaluable internal and external asset. Satisfy your nerves by enough personal production. Train your nerves to do what YOU want by constant self-suggestion, relax the nerves at the proper time by distraction, by a good personal philosophy, by direct command.

Your nerves are only too glad to serve you, to take orders from you, just as soon as you show you understand them and are willing to respect their rights, too.

A well balanced nervous system, too, will directly aid the body in gaining and maintaining health. Coolness under fire, control and perspective are characteristics that win you a reputation for reliability. They also bring a vast amount of personal content.

6. GRADE UP!

Off hand you'll say affectation is wrong. Look into it and you'll find that *real* affectation is *right*.

The thing generally called "affectation" is only false affectation.

A person puts on a tone of voice that is not natural, not in keeping with other characteristics of the person. The act is called "affectation." Actually it was only an attempt at affectation, a miserable attempt. Because *consistency* is lacking.

True affectation is one of the most worthy acts of man. It has two essentials: First, *grading up;* second, *consistency*.

You have the right to be discontented with imperfection, with disorder, with commonness, cheapness, and strife. These things belong to the lower level of human existence. When you seek to rise above that level, you are affecting a role other than the one that was yours formerly. That's affectation—and you have every right to grade yourself up.

But in the act of grading up, be consistent! You can hardly do any single new thing without involving a whole new world of related things that also must be handled in terms of the new level. For instance, if you decide to pronounce "either" as *eyether,* you have every right to do so and you should be commended, provided you agree to pronounce every other word in the English language which is under the influence of the *eyether* affectation, that is, as those other words which are so pronounced by the people to whom *eyether* is *not* an affectation. But if you don't know what those other words so affected are, for goodness' sake, keep on calling it *either!*

We spot affectation in another by his inconsistency. Inconsistency is the death of affectation. On the other hand, when you last met a new person who apparently has "affected ways" how alert you were to catch the first mistake he or she made. That mistake would have been an inconsistency. But if the person went on, in apparently outlandish and overstrained fashion, and DID NOT MAKE ANY MISTAKE, he began to command your respect, and you began to question yourself as to whether his way was not better. For if the thing is on a higher plane, and it's handled consistently, it inspires the audience to a much higher appreciation and becomes affectation in the true meaning of the word.

You can easily *grade up* in all of your human habits and activities. If you dress better, dress better in every detail. If you stand straighter, stand straighter *always* not just when you think of it. If you should use better English, use better English in every situation—at home with the children, and at the factory talking to men in overalls. When you grade up, you can't be all things to all people—but you can be *right* and whether others want to follow that *right* or not, you can win their respect by simply remaining *consistent!*

Seek the finer things, act the better way, *grade up!* As an ensemble, as a complete whole, all parts of which match perfectly. Never be ashamed of using a big word, if that word is the right word. Never avoid it *because* it's big. If it's the *right* word, even though it's *big,* you *have* to use it! For in grading up every turn in the road is a crisis; failure to keep on means ruin, inconsistency brings ridicule and derision, and to fear to grade up is the worst inconsistency of all.

Ability

1. HOW'S YOUR GREY MATTER?

The greatest of all ability is the ability to think.

What is thought? Look back to the last time you were trying to "think." You might have held your head in your hands and said, "Let me think." What were you trying to do then? You were simply trying to get some of the marks, or points, or characteristics of an object or event into your mind.

That is thought. Thought is the ability to abstract the nature of the thing from the thing and hold it in your mind. There it was in the thing or subject. Now you draw it away from the thing and you hold it in your own mind. It belongs to you. It is your thought.

183

Thought, or this abstracting power of the mind, to be effective requires the power of definition. To think about a thing, you must be able to recognize how far the thing goes, you must know its boundaries. When you are able to define what anything is, that is, *state everything it is and exclude everything it is not,* then and not until then are you really able to think!

After defining the thing, break it into its parts. Number these parts, 1, 2, 3, and so on. Every enumeration is impressive and aids understanding. Be able to list the parts in order of sequence and in order of importance.

Know the beginning, middle, and end of every subject. Know the relation of these parts to one another.

Thought is not just an idle activity of the mind. Thought is intended to be *used.* In other words, the end of thought is *efficiency.*

Tie your thought to efficiency always! The easiest way to keep thought and efficiency interlocked is to keep asking yourself these two questions:

1. What am I trying to do?
2. How am I trying to do it?

Every problem, every activity, every job is subject to the scorching scrutiny of these two mild, simple questions. Use them in the midst of great deliberations, important conferences, where to ask them out loud is to wield the mightiest power of drama, use them in the quiet of your own solitary meditation, to guide you to the next move, to force you to an honest answer.

If you care to be known as a man who can think, let people hear you ask these questions everlastingly: "What are we trying to do? How are we trying to do it?"

2. CUT OUT THE RED TAPE

True efficiency consists in reducing the required amount of work for a definite amount of production to an absolute minimum.

Don't do the unnecessary thing.

Don't do work that nobody uses.

Don't double your tracks, that is, don't do the same work over twice.

Use the work already being done, whether it be a natural force such as the wind used to turn a windmill or sail a ship, or a personal force, such as the post-office system that will carry a letter thousands of miles for 3 cents. (You couldn't do it yourself for that!)

The universal marks of efficiency are *brevity, compactness, speed, utility.* In practically all the work you do, you can assume that there is a definite measure of utility. Now if you will save the usefulness, ALL the usefulness, and keep it *brief,* you will reduce your production time amazingly, cut the cost, deliver the full force of every ounce of energy expended. You will be efficient.

Such efficiency is quiet, simple. It never lends itself to publicity or advertising. Let efficiency advertise itself, never attempt to call attention to it. Advertising, so useful in many other things, simply calls efficiency into question, and ultimately ruins it. Efficiency and hot air don't mix! One destroys the other!

8. DON'T SAY "I THINK"

The essence of accuracy is evidence. In a law court, the lawyer who cross examines you refuses even to allow you to start a statement with "I think." He does not want your opinion. Your opinion is not evidence.

If only people's opinions and fallacious conclusions were omitted from every business conference, how much easier would it be to get at the facts, and how many more facts would come to the surface!

But no! They must start every statement with "I think," "In my judgment," "My idea is" and a hundred other preambles that are equivalent to saying, "The information I am now giving you is NOT ACCURATE."

The person who honors reliability and puts its need in first place, as most sensible men do, even though the world at large does not, will demand that you be accurate. His spoken or unspoken questions are:

What?
Where?
How?
When?
Why?
How much?
Of what kind?
Under what circumstances?

186

Witnessed by?
Recorded by?
On what authority?

Notice how mere you, your emotions and your opinions have no place in the scheme whatever. When you are an accurate man, you are simply a reporter of facts. It is asked of you that you have access to the facts, by reason of being on hand when they were presented, or by reason of your ability to find, to isolate, a fact already established by someone else's authority or by an automatic system of recording which is purely mechanical and not personal.

You may step outside on a bitter cold morning and say, "Gee! It must be at least zero!" Actually it may be fifteen above, by the correct thermometer. And that inanimate instrument becomes a much more substantial source of truth than you—a living being! You have often guessed at the time and been an hour or half an hour off. The watch's report was ever so much better than your guess!

After all, if your opinion refers to so-called facts, but is only an opinion, it becomes nothing more than a guess. The guesser is the most inaccurate man on the face of the globe. Nobody respects him, nobody depends on him.

4. REMEMBER?

Perhaps the most universally popular mark of reliability is a good memory. You can astonish people by simply remembering things about them, things they said or did, things that happened to them, their likes, dislikes, hobbies, their fears and worries. Because everyone is so wrapped up in himself, and subconsciously knows no one else cares about him, he is practically overcome when you show him you remember something that concerned him intimately.

This is, of course, the "selling side" of a good memory. A good memory has many mechanical advantages that are perhaps more important when considered strictly under the subject of reliability. Memory helps you retain the knowledge you have acquired, facts, and dates, that can be useful in making quick decisions and in saving time and delay.

A memory for dates, telephone numbers, names and street addresses makes a startling impression on people —because most people have poor memories. Memory instantly identifies you as a reliable man.

Here are a few ways to acquire a good memory— and it is essential that you realize that no matter how old you now are, or how poor your memory is, you can acquire a splendid memory in quick time with a little practice of the memory rules:

a. Pay attention. Apply yourself to the speaker, to the action. Observe, listen, concentrate. Do everything to prevent distractions as soon as they may occur. You know very well that when you HAD to remember, when you WANTED to remember, you could remember. You remember because you PAY ATTENTION. Unless you do pay attention all memory is impossible.

b. Memorize it. This is perhaps the way you learned everything at school, and doubtless the only things you remembered are those that you memorized best. To memorize, say the thing over and over. Say it a hundred times. Say it out loud. Say it with your lips. Say it mentally. Constant repetition will make it a part of your innermost self, your subconscious mind will take it up and hold on to it forever. Memory teachers may state that memorizing is the wrong way to remember, but *it's a way that you know,* and it's a way that will surely bring results! Even without paying attention, if you just repeat the thing, automatically, mechanically, you will remember it!

c. Association. At the time the thing to be remembered is happening, something else is happening too. Think of the two things together and one thing later will remind you of the other. Or any fact, name or thing can be associated with something that happened long ago, and by tying the two things together the mind is better able to recall the new thing. Association can be thus made, for memory purpose, through similarity of time, appearance, sound, smell, consequences, antecedents, nature, or through partial similarity of the same elements. Perhaps the cleanest cut association is the association of sequence. "This thing followed that thing, flowed out of it!" And so the cause is remembered by the effect and the effect by the cause.

d. Exaggeration. All things that were given unusual stress, spotlighting, or importance we remember long. To exaggerate an object mentally, to make a cat bigger than a house, makes it easy for the mind to recall the cat.

e. Motion. An object in motion causes the eye to follow it, requires that attention be paid to it. Make a mental picture of the object in motion, such as a house flying, a balloon exploding, and the forced attention insures automatic memory.

Be known as the man with a memory. Your memory will be constantly used for information and confirmation, and through your good memory your reliability will be well established.

5. MOVE IN FASTER COMPANY

There was a time when you started to play some kind of game. You might have dubbed along at it for some time, getting nowhere, showing only slight improvement. Then you were thrown among, or worked your way into, a crowd which played the game much better than you, much better than you had ever hoped to play.

Pretty soon after that you registered a marked improvement, and were making an excellent showing even among these expert players.

The cause? *You had moved into faster company.* You learn much faster as soon as you move into faster company.

If you would advance socially, work your way into the best layer of society. Don't tell yourself it is over your head. Don't say it is impossible of attainment. Don't wonder how you would act if you ever got there.

Just go out and figure a way of breaking in. You may
have to sit on the fringe for a while, but you can get
in if you want to. And if society means something to
you why not avail yourself of the best?

The same way with education. Your education is
never completed, and unless it is being increased it
surely is being depleted. No educated man can improve
his education by associating with the uneducated masses,
by constantly giving away his education and receiving
no educational recompense in return. He may acquire
new knowledge and understanding, it is true, but if he
seeks betterment of his formal education he should
arrange to mix with people even better educated than
he. The words, the thoughts, the mental refinements of
these people will pile new educational development on
him.

If you would be better in the craft you are following, in the particular department of business activity at
which you make a living, *move in faster company!* Find
out who are the very best men in your line, arrange
to meet them, get to know them intimately and comprehensively. Find out their theories, their special devices
for skill, their opinions of coming trends, grab the benefit of their advanced thinking and make it your very
own.

Just to move in faster company is to double your
ability overnight. But it's important that you know
what to do when you move in. First, *act as if you really
belong!* Under no circumstances confess that you are
an amateur or a greenhorn; act just as easy, just as

nonchalant, just as competently as any of the others.

Second, to gain this easy composure quickly, *watch your form!* Form is everything no matter what the activity. Don't be afraid or ashamed to do a little posing. You are guilty of just as much affectation in proclaiming your deficiencies as you are in acting as if you are a pro. Act in form.

Third, *keep your eyes open!* Observe. Pay attention. You have worked your way into the big league, now make it count! Watch how the big leaguers carry themselves. There seems to be a set routine, a real convention to the business. They all go through a certain number of motions; nobody misses. There must be something to it, too (even though you don't see it right now). So believe blindly, and *you* do the same things. While you're getting there don't be backward at imitation. Imitating is the fastest way to climb, and if you're following good examples you can't go wrong.

What is faster company? It is the group, the body, the set of individuals, that common agreement of people at large places at the top of a given profession or activity. The common acceptance may never be exactly or exclusively right, but it certainly is never wrong, and its authority is the best means of discovering the faster company. There may be better ball players than the American and National League players, there may be better fighters than the respective champions in the different classes, but it's very hard to find them. Common acceptance, right away, tells you where the faster company is!

Move in faster company! Get class by associating with class. By all means *avoid* the hams, the dolts, the boneheads. If you are moved by the impulse to teach them, to reform them, to lift them up, forsake that impulse—*for you never can!* Make it your business to mix with people who are smarter, cleverer, more advanced than you—and you be the one that's lifted up.

6. THE SOURCE OF ALL ABILITY—STRAIGHT THINKING

Your mind, with its power to reason, is the first source of all your ability. The rules under which your reason works are known as the laws of logic.

Because so little is generally known about logic and because so much false logic is used in our business, social and economic existence, it is highly imperative, if you are going to do *a complete job* of putting yourself over, that you master logic in all its workings. There are few things as thrilling as a logical mind in action, and nothing commercially is quite so valuable as the conclusions that flow from logical analysis. If you can make yourself a straight thinker, you can quickly acquire all the arts needed for success.

Let's look briefly into the basic doctrines of logic with a view of picking up skill in its use.

7. LOGIC

Logic is the system which shows you *how* to think and tells you how to determine the *truth of what you think.*

Reasoning or proof is simply the operation of law. There are two kinds of reasoning. First kind is *deduction*, the basis of which is this simple law which all men agree on:

The whole includes all or any of its parts; but no part can ever equal the whole.

Example:

Every chair has a seat;
This piece of furniture is a chair;
Therefore, it has a seat.

The *whole,* which is chair, includes the *part,* which is seat. When the evidence shows that some new thing is a chair, it automatically becomes the *whole,* and it must *include* seat. The above deduction therefore is a good proof, simple because it obeys the law regarding the whole and its parts, and *not* because it *sounds* like a proof.

For here is a combination of statements that sound like proof, but are not:

Every chair has a seat;
This piece of furniture has a seat;
Therefore, it is a chair.

In each of the first two statements seat is a *part* of chair, while chair is the *whole,* and since we have agreed that part can never equal whole, seat can't equal chair. No connecting link has been established between the first statement and the third statement, and, therefore, though it *sounds* like logic, it cannot be admitted as true.

We see now that in all cases where we reason by deduction, there must be a *connection* between the different statements by which we attempt to arrive at a conclusion. In all cases this connection turns out to be the *whole of the thing,* being represented somewhere in each of the two statements or premises. If the whole has been represented and connected by occurring twice, then we must admit something about the part that is dragged in. If, however, no connection has been made, between the first statement and the second, no deduction is possible, as:

Every chair has a seat;
Monday follows Sunday;
Therefore, fire is hot.

Though the third statement is undoubtedly true, it is no deduction, because it is not the part of anything nor the whole of anything, and in no way refers to the only rule of deduction, namely, the whole includes any and all of its parts, but, under no circumstances, can a part ever equal the whole.

The law must be expressed before a deduction can be established! No matter how logical the deduction may sound, it is no deduction until it expresses that fun-

195

damental law. Even so pretty a piece of "reasoning" as this, therefore,

> We put on the new advertising campaign;
> Sales immediately jumped 100 per cent;
> Therefore, the advertising caused the sales—

must be discarded as being just as silly, inappropriate and illegitimate as the "Every chair has a seat; Monday follows Sunday; Therefore, fire is hot" combination.

You say: "But the advertising DID cause the sales!" We say, "But FIRE IS HOT!" Just because the third statement is true, doesn't make it a deduction. It must follow deduction's immutable law.

There's a second kind of reasoning known as INDUCTION, and its fundamental law is this:

> All of the parts put together must equal the whole.

Induction is either *Complete* or *Incomplete*. It is *Complete* when we actually get all of the parts and put them together. For instance:

> Water is a liquid containing two parts of hydrogen and one part of oxygen and nothing else, and it is the only liquid so made up.

> Now we get ahold of two parts of hydrogen and one part of oxygen, cause them to unite and we make a liquid. Just these three parts

are represented, nothing else; therefore, the
liquid we have just made must be water.

All of the parts put together must equal the whole!
Incomplete induction is based on a variation of this
same rule, the variation may be stated thus:

> If all the requisite parts of an action always
> equal the action when they are assembled, if
> experiment shows they have never failed to
> equal this action, and if the experiment is
> enacted a large enough number of times, then
> the whole action may be predicted and posi-
> tively known in advance of the parts actually
> being put together.

If you hold a baseball in your hand, and releasing
tension of your fingers let it drop to the ground a thousand times, if it has never failed to drop to the ground
even once, then you can positively know that if you
put together the same parts or requisites a million times
more, the baseball will drop to the ground on each of
the million times. It will not be necessary to go through
the million experiments: *Your incomplete experience*
constitutes full and satisfying proof!

Such are the simple rules of logical conclusions; no
other rules are necessary, no others apply, and if any
others are introduced, the conclusions, no matter right
or wrong, cannot be honored!

But to prevent confusion and to insure an airtight

application of the rules, the things we are talking about —the whole and its parts—must be *defined* and the terms as defined be understood clearly and agreed on by all.

A definition must be exact, legal, all inclusive, all exclusive. It can't be a mere description, a meaning, a synonym, an illustration. It must be a *definition*.

A definition is a statement about a thing which includes everything the thing is and everything falling in its special class and excludes everything the thing is not.

If the terms in any proof are thus defined and agreed on, and the laws of deduction and induction observed, ALL THE CONCLUSIONS MUST BE HONORED!

Notice, that we didn't say "granted." For to grant any conclusion must involve conceding the TRUTH of the premises in addition to their proper sequence.

How do you know what is true and what is not true? One more simple rule:

The standard by which you judge truth is objective evidence.

Truth is not determined by your own subjective desires, your own subjective feelings, your opinions, your guesses, your second-hand reports. Truth is WHAT ACTUALLY IS—regardless of anyone's wishes, opinions, prayers, contradictions, prejudices or regrets. Remember when someone near and dear to you died? You didn't want that dear one dead, you cried to heaven not to believe it, but you had to admit it. Why? *Because the evidence showed the person was dead.*

Objective evidence! The simple, cold, uncolored facts

as they happened and as they were reported mechanically and impartially! Of course, these facts, this evidence, must in the end be furnished by human testimony—some human being records and presents them, for man is the only animal able to keep records. Such testimony involves two essentials:

1. That the witness, reporter, or recorder was at the place at the time the thing was happening, that he was competent and in full possession of his faculties of perception, which were healthy and normally applied to the things that were happening.

2. That he could have no motive for deception, trickery, falsifying or prejudice; and that there could be no motive involved by any other agent in the situation to deceive him.

On such hard rules as these are men sent to the electric chair! And though we little realize it, all of the great truths of life are accepted, automatically by us, according to this simple system of direct evidence.

You pass a house. You look up. You see the house. The day is clear. Your eyes are normal. You know a house when you see one. No one could have any reason for fooling you. The evidence is in. *The thing is a house!*

By deduction and induction we reason from known premises to previously unknown conclusions which were really contained in the premises. By the laws of evidence we check the premises to be sure they are true. If the *form* of your thinking is correct and the *content* true, you are that rare and honorable being, *a logical man.*

8. THE CULTIVATION OF ABILITY

Thus we see that the source of all ability is logic, and true logic must always be protected from the false.

Logic delivers the truth to you, but what are you going to do with the truth? The answer is *practice.* The first way to acquire skill and efficiency, once you possess knowledge, is *practice.* The greatest of all professionals are the most faithful exponents of practice, honest, patient drudgery in executing and repeating the truths they have learned theoretically.

Practice renders its greatest returns when accompanied by active theory. If you would be a good student and an apt pupil, always have a personal theory you are experimenting with. Then as you proceed to practice, proceed to prove or disprove your theory. Soon your hand, your brain, and your mind merge to become one competent *actor,* and *you possess ability!*

Conservativeness

1. THE TRICK OF UNDERSTATEMENT

Non-exaggeration is the soul of all conservativeness. Nearly everyone is guilty of exaggeration and overstatement, and our natural impulse on listening to any plus or positive statement by another, is to discount it at least 50 per cent.

We generally find that ensuing events proved the discount was not too stringent.

What a pleasant relief, in the midst of all the superlatives and unsubstantial promises, to find someone who minimizes, who actually understates the amount and the quality of the goodness that is there or about to be delivered. This is the person we call RELIABLE, even though he is guilty of the error of minimizing the actual truth.

The old adage says: "Anticipation is greater than realization." But what a scoop, what a boom, what a sensation, when things turn out even better than we anticipated!

You can now see that to be conservative by understating should make quite a popular idol out of you. Let events, reaching a much lustier volume than you predicted, prove you were wrong—the people will all INSIST YOU WERE RIGHT! They will look on you as their greatest benefactor; your personality will be invested with surprise, showmanship, power, and reliability.

And wonder of wonders—whenever you understate afterwards—your every understatement will be flowering with promise, with encouragement and anticipation, for people will feel they are *sure to collect* what you predict *and get a great deal more besides!* When you cut down on the truth, you really add to it.

2. THINK BEFORE YOU ANSWER

If you would be considered reliable, think before you answer questions, think before you make any definite statements.

The world is full of people who pride themselves on how fast they can answer a question. They tear off the answer almost as fast as the question is asked, without thinking, without reflecting, and generally *without any basis!* They seem to believe that the answer can't be considered reliable, nor they competent, unless it is given quickly.

Reliable people, on the other hand, don't answer quickly. They think. If they make definite statements, they distinguish them or qualify them so that they will be exact. As you wait for the answer, you just seem to know it will be sound and reliable. And the pause guarantees extra attention from you.

The smart alecks, the glib know-it-alls, the fast talkers *always have an answer.* Sometimes the reliable man hasn't; if he doesn't know the answer to the question, he says: "I don't know," and somehow, out of that singular confession of ignorance, the questions he does answer take on an added reliability.

Always use your oral faculties for the purpose for which they were intended. They weren't given to you just for the sake of making noise like the parrot or the dog. They were intended to be used in expressing the thoughts in your head. Before you throw your tongue into gear be sure you have your thoughts in hand. It will require a brief pause before you answer the question. *Think before you answer!*

Self-Confidence

1. SELL YOURSELF TO YOURSELF

In preparing the material for this book, I talked personally to thousands of salesmen, business leaders and psychologists. I asked them all the same question:

"What is the first quality a man needs in order
to sell himself to others?"

The unanimity of response was astonishing. They practically all said: "Self-confidence!"

And yet here you find the grand quality of Self-Confidence listed under Reliability, number Seven in a list of Eight!

In one respect, self-confidence might be considered a department of Egotism, which is a subdivision of Expression. But I insist it belongs under Reliability because it is one of the surest means for creating in others a feeling of reliability in you.

If you're self-confident, you're a reliable man!

Self-confidence comes first from selling yourself to yourself on your product or proposition. It is a part of reliability simply because it's primarily based on truth.

To sell yourself on anything, first seek the truth, the right, the excellence in the thing. No man can really sell himself on something cheap, false, or wrong. If you will study the thing you are going to sell, seeking out its basic truth, and the genuine merit behind it, you will eventually find complete justification for your being engaged in selling it.

Continue to contemplate this merit, till it becomes big, lusty, and comparable to the merit of any rival product or proposition. The longer you gaze at the truth, the more convinced you are that you might fight to uphold it. This conviction gets itself across immediately to whomever you speak, even though that person does not immediately see the justification for your feeling the way you do. But if *you're* sold on the proposition, he will be sold by the very fact that *you're* sold.

Every proposition or product, excepting those things which are deliberately dishonest, has some fundamental merit to it. This fundamental merit is the all important thing in your life. Never let it be trampled under foot. Never let it be ridiculed by a clever comparison. Fight to uphold it with the same patriotism that you show for the flag of your country. The genuineness of your fervor cannot then be resisted.

It's easy to develop self-confidence. *Simply know you're right.*

The continued repetition and reflection on this knowledge keeps your self-confidence alive forever. Self-confidence creates trust in the heart of the man you're selling; it helps him make up his mind; it convinces him that his money or his support will be safe with you. For he knows blindly, but none the less certainly, that there can never be self-confidence unless it is backed by truth. It is the world's noblest concession to the nobility of truth that it votes for the man who is sure he's right.

2. THAT "AIR OF ASSURANCE"

At some time or another you've had trouble with some part of your house. The plumbing, the electrical circuit. Maybe a door wouldn't close or a key wouldn't turn in the lock.

A mechanic was called in, and immediately on his entrance you watched him like a hawk. It seems you had already dabbled a little in trying to fix the trouble yourself—so you knew something about the conditions he had to face. As the mechanic addressed his task, in those first few minutes you were watching him, you were secretly deciding whether he knew anything or not.

What was it about him that won your respect or drew your censure? It was *the way he carried himself.* If he acted weak or uncertain, if he scratched his head in puzzlement, if he asked you a lot of foolish questions, if he poked around in an amateurish way, if he rushed for his tools frantically without stopping to analyze the trouble first, then you KNEW he was no mechanic at all, and you had no belief the trouble would be properly eliminated.

But if the man carried about him AN AIR OF ASSUR-ANCE, if he was cool and unhurried, if he paused to drop a word or two to make you feel at ease, why you *did* suddenly feel at ease; the case was in good hands!

205

Lawyers, doctors, manufacturers, all business men would do well to acquire that priceless element in public relations, *a self-assured air!* No one is going to feel confident in you, unless you first feel confident in yourself! If you can give off this air of quiet self-confidence, if you can make it "second nature," you will find all people flocking to you, relying on you, trusting you implicitly.

Now the test of self-confidence is not essentially *experience.* Anyone who has done a given thing a number of times is bound to feel confident when he meets that same thing again. You are not going to get flustered or rattled over an experience you have already been through, a thing you *know.* What throws you out of gear, is *the thing that never came up before.* The new thing! The strange thing! The foreign, complex, dangerous thing! You meet it—and if you are not on your guard—your fear and excitement immediately show on your face, in your words and actions. The person with whom you're dealing instantly senses your panic, loses all confidence in anything you may do from that point on!

At all costs, hold on to that "air of assurance"! Hold on to it ESPECIALLY at the moment when you are anything *but* self-assured. It's perfectly all right to see the danger, the tangle, the hopelessness of a situation. See it inwardly, but don't acknowledge it out loud. Carry yourself with coolness, calmness, assurance. Let your man feel that "everything is going to come out ALL RIGHT."

When you comport yourself this way, a miracle suddenly happens! You are confident (even without justification). This confidence that you have created—and preserved—artificially and strictly for the sake of impression, now begins to work on yourself! The thing that baffled you clears up! The fright vanishes! In a flash you get the inspiration that furnishes the solution to the whole problem. *You win by being confident.*

You wouldn't keep on going to a doctor who was uncertain about what ailed you. Well, you're the other fellow's doctor. Be confident, and show it. Never drop that precious "air of assurance."

☆

Persuasiveness

Here is the final quality needed to get you across the street, out of danger of fierce miscellaneous traffic and into the market place of brilliant personality. *Persuasiveness is the ability to get people to do what you want them to do.*

It is of two kinds: Direct and Indirect.

Direct Persuasiveness

1. "HIGH PRESSURE"

You get the other man to act by *forcing* him to act. In this system, the hand is heavy, the way is sometimes cruel; but, properly applied, direct persuasiveness is very effective. The time will come when you have to use it, so it's well to know some of its principles.

209

2. GETTING OTHERS INVOLVED IN YOUR PROJECTS

If you are a married man, you will recall that, almost immediately after you were married, you began to make more money. Enforced participation in a stiffer economic existence caused you to do the necessary things to improve your income. If you hadn't been married you probably wouldn't have done those things.

Today's manner of living has done much to destroy people's initiative and productivity. Radio, for example, is the direct foe of reading, because all radio requires is the flipping of a switch, while reading is strain both on the eyes and the brain. In reading there is some call for active work. Listening to the radio—by now the chief pastime of a hundred million Americans—is no work at all.

Consequently, people won't do a thing until they are *forced* into it. They delay, they put off, they forget. Their sense perceptions are dulled, their bodies and minds strangled into passivity. Any plan which requires their active participation, must have a threat, a penalty. Non-action must be met with embarrassment, financial or personal; their minds must be made up for them; the scheme must be so constructed that they simply cannot withdraw.

Example: In a given office there are perhaps forty people who write letters, personal letters, form letters. Some of these letter writers are executives, some are junior correspondents. The concern pleads with every letter writer to improve his letters, to think, to use better copy, to put salesmanship and enthusiasm into them. All to no avail. Then an idea. A prize of $50 is offered to the man, no matter what his position, who writes the best letter in a given month. All letter writers are required to submit what they considered the six best letters they have written that month to a jury composed of the officers of the concern. Each man knows he must present six, so he bears down in making *all* his letters better. The high executive sees to it that he won't be outdistanced by the junior correspondent while the latter gets positively brilliant at being given this chance to score a triumph. And yet it is all done under the disguise of *generosity,* the $50 prize. The stunt, which is all leverage through fear of embarrassment, draws about $10,000 worth of extra effort out of all concerned!

Public Commitment—If a man commits himself publicly to a certain promise, he is forced to make good on the promise. Advertising men often published at the bottom of an advertisement, "One of a series of fifteen," thus committing the advertiser to the program. Many a football player doesn't quit, merely because so many people are watching him. Privately a million people quit every day who would never quit if they were doing the same thing in public.

If another gives you a promise, it is good strategy to announce publicly what he is going to do. With the event given such publicity he is "persuaded" not to back down on his resolution.

Requiring the Complement—The camera is useless without the film, the razor without the blade. The fish bait calls for the purchase of tackle, the ammunition needs a gun to shoot it off. See that your man gets *part*—with some other part still needed. He will be automatically forced into buying that other part.

Get His Money in It—The fellow who buys a book is more likely to read it than if it be given to him free. Concerns offer to pay for half the cost of sales courses for their men; they would gladly pay all but they know that when the man's own money is in it, he will work all the harder to get something out of it.

A Cash Deposit—Also helps to enforce participation. Once they put some of their money into it, they generally go all the way through.

Get Him Started—Get the man started! Get him part way into the action. Generally the start itself is enough to shake up the molecules of energy inside him which will keep him going from that point on. Organizations believe in giving their members *exercise,* such as community singing, parades, drills, business meetings. Participation breeds still further participation, so sample the participation early!

3. MAKE YOURSELF INDISPENSABLE TO THE "BOSS"

The mother means so much to the baby, because the mother is food, care, and attention. When the child becomes the adult, and is able to support himself, mother knows he is getting away from her simply because she at this point is not indispensable and necessary to his existence.

Contrive to make yourself a necessary part of any action, project, or service in which you have a selfish role. People will do what you want, when they *have* to do what you want! If your fame is all dominant in a particular field, they simply *have* to put you on the program! If you are the only man who can do a certain type of work, they *have* to come to you!

You've often heard it said of a man: "He's not in the picture!" What is meant is that the man isn't necessary. Here are a few ways to give yourself the indispensable quality that counts you into the schemes where you want to be.

1. Develop a rare and special skill. If that skill is part of the scheme, and you are the only one who has it, you must be admitted.

2. Count yourself in. Just declare yourself in, and at the first opportunity take in your hands a vital department of the project, with its records, its methods, its plans and direction.

3. Spoil them with service. Give your customers or those you are seeking to influence so much genuine help and comfortable service that they will be lost if you aren't on hand to do it.

4. Hold the purse strings. If it's your money running the project, dish it out sparingly so that they have to keep coming to you. If it's not your money, talk the money at every opportunity, emphasize the importance of care and economy, so that you are tied in inseparably with the expenditure of money.

5. Make your endorsement valuable. By keeping in

the center of things, people will want to know how you stand on a given issue. Put some importance to your endorsement by only endorsing quality things. That will make your name much more valuable, and consequently very necessary to the contemplated activity.

4. ASK

Persuasion, sometimes, is simply a matter of *asking*. If you don't ask, you may get nothing. If you do ask, you ought to know how to ask.

1. Gauge your man. Find out if the person from whom you are asking is liberal, generous, pliable. If he doesn't know how to say "No," ask him in just about any way you want, and your request will be granted.

2. Catch him in good humor. Never go after a favor when the man who could grant it is in bad humor. Make inquiries from other people about the state of his disposition. Find out, if you can, whether some extremely favorable things have been happening to him. Then as you approach him with your request, first *sound him out,* not hurling the request at him forthright, but talking about other things first to determine if he is in a pleasant frame of mind.

3. Determine whether you have anything to lose by asking. If the man has to say No to you, is he or you or both going to lose something? If so, don't ask, at least not until you have modeled circumstances more strategically. If you have nothing to lose by his saying No and a possibility of his saying Yes go ahead and ask!

4. Is he obligated to say Yes? If you want a Yes from the man and you have so obligated him previously that he cannot say No, first wait to see if he'll say Yes voluntarily, if not, ask him for it directly!

5. GET THE NAME ON THE DOTTED LINE

People have the best of intentions. People are influenced by suggestion and good salesmanship. They're "sold." And yet they SIMPLY WILL NOT ACT. They are too lazy to do anything but O.K. the proposition mentally, and then proceed to forget all about it.

Don't stop your persuasion at "having done a good job." Get the name on the dotted line. Ask for the favor —do it smoothly, do it adroitly, but truly ASK FOR IT. Put the pressure on, invisibly, of course, but let it be pressure nevertheless! You can't lose by making a definite stand.

6. USE THE DEADLINE

People invariably let their bills ride until discount day; then they know that if that day passes they lose money. So they act.

They don't buy their automobile licenses for the new year until the police begin arresting them or when a deadline is announced.

If railroad trains and steamships didn't leave at *exactly* the time announced—a great many people would miss connections. Now hardly anyone is ever late. The companies define the deadline *clearly.*

215

If church is to start at nine o'clock, start it at nine o'clock exactly. Don't wait. Don't delay in hopes that you'll accommodate more latecomers. Because the less distinct the deadline is, the more latecomers you have; but once they know—having had the actual proof of being late half a minute after the deadline—they will have a great deal more respect for the deadline.

The deadline is no deadline, unless it is definite, clear, and the same for all; it must be acknowledged and handled with railroad accuracy!

If you have announced that a proposition will be withdrawn after a certain date, WITHDRAW IT, once and for all. Don't compromise, don't extend, and the next time the deadline is announced they will act in plenty of time.

Things are done when THEY HAVE TO BE DONE. There's no necessity so compelling as the necessity for acting in time.

7. THE VALUE OF MAKING A NUISANCE OUT OF YOURSELF

Never take No from anybody; make a pest of yourself till you finally shake out of your man the thing you are seeking.

There are those who say that pestiness is undiplomatic, tactless. It is. But it has been known to work where tact and politeness were futile. In fact, tact and politeness used in an abundant degree very often end in nothing, but an abundance of pestiness always gets results.

Pestiness is simply the quality of keeping after the other man until he gives you what you want. The world's greatest pests are children; and the pestier they are the more often they get what they're after.

Of course, the pesty way is the hard way, *but it's a way*. When all other things fail, it's the only way.

Pestiness feeds on the word NO. The champion pest gobbles up that word NO like it was corn on the cob. He knows it's meant for him, he expects it. As he relentlessly follows you up, you sometimes suspect that he would be disappointed if you said Yes; in fact, the way the sad, uneven contest ends is that you do decide to disappoint him and say Yes—and to your great surprise find that it was Yes the pest wanted after all. But your concession was certainly worth the relief of being rid of him.

If *you* give in to the pest, and, understand, I mean the real pest, the pest that can't be shaken, insulted, hid from—so will *others* give in to you when you assume the pest role. Of course, I don't recommend you become a pest except as a last resort. But when all other tricks of selling yourself fail—as they sometimes may— through misappropriateness or misapplication—don't fail to fall back on this ace in the hole: *Be a pest.*

As a pest you will be temporarily despised, but finally honored. They will start out by hating you, but wind up by liking you!

Be sure to earn the distinction of being the pest who *sticks till he wins*—don't be the kind of pest who quits pestering under pressure of heavy protest or refusal.

217

Indirect Persuasiveness

1. THE SIX ANCIENT FOES OF PERSUASION

The indirect nature of persuasiveness suggests that you be adroit, soothing, smooth.

Speak in a low voice. In this field you can't persuade by shouting out loud in a heated argument.

Take what you consider your best argument or suggestion, and controlling your excitement, erase your emphasis, and deliberately pitch your voice several tones lower than you originally planned. The low voice will keep you cool, and put all of your wallop where it should be—in the psychological force of your suggestions and motives.

But before you attempt to persuade anyone, take into account these age-old resistances which are imbedded in the minds and emotions of all people.

Suspicion.

Most people suspect that you have an ulterior purpose, that your motives are shady and untrustworthy. As long as this suspicion remains in their minds, your progress at persuading can't advance a single inch.

Dissolve suspicion by laying your cards on the table. By showing all the facts. By honestly admitting your selfish advantage. By showing the unfavorable side of the thing and answering objections before they are raised by the other man.

Inertia.

The universal sin of all mankind is laziness. People simply will not move, will not budge, even to do themselves a favor. They may make up their minds but their bodies refuse to function in order to furnish the final action. They stay put. Stick to habit.

Dissolve inertia with YOUR OWN SPIRIT. Spirit is contagious, spirit is full of life force, spirit can instantly turn a weak vegetable into a dynamic human being. Turn on the spirit. Get hot! Vibrate! Become intense!

Fear.

You're afraid, I'm afraid, everybody's afraid. The two principal fears are the fear of being killed and the fear of being ridiculed. The life preservation instinct causes people to hold on to their money, when they might otherwise invest it in you, your cause, or your product. The instinct to avoid the scars of ridicule prevents them from participating in public events, from appearing in the spotlight, from taking the initiative.

Dissolve fear by showing a little consideration. You can't reason anybody out of fear, but you can show them sympathy and thus make the fear a little less important. Let the other know that you, too, have been afraid, are still afraid of many things. Understand this fear before you start to minimize it. Feel like he does about it and you'll quickly get just the right idea for losing that fear.

219

Pride.

How many of your associates and acquaintances are too hard to handle? Too proud, too stubborn to buy from you, to receive a well meant suggestion, to join with you in your objective. These are the people who "can't be sold anything."

Dissolve pride by glorifying it. Build up that proud, stubborn individual!

Go to extra length to show him your respect and honor. He may then condescend to be persuaded!

Incompetency.

Some people are apparently not worth persuading, because they haven't the money to buy, even if they wanted to, they haven't the force, the standing or the authority to contribute tangible help to you. Seems like you oughtn't to fool with them at all!

Dissolve incompetency by giving it IMPORTANCE. If the man hasn't the money, sell him anyhow. If he's sold well enough he may raise the money among his relatives or friends. If he hasn't any standing or authority, treat him with the utmost attention and respect, act toward him as if he were a man of great importance. The goodwill you create in him may quickly be forwarded to the person who really has the authority. No one is too small for you to ignore. When you're truly immersed in the goodness of your own proposition, you are not choosy about whom you sell. Sell EVERYBODY!

Jealousy.

Few people who started on the same basis as others can bear to see themselves outdistanced by those others. In persuasion you may have to play one person against the other, for envy and jealousy have a driving force of millions of horsepower. Everybody secretly wants to "keep up with the Joneses."

2. FIND THE ANGLE AND SPEED THE SALE

Veteran schemers, in starting any particular plan intended to capture a definite prize, have a pet question they always ask in discussing the project: "What's the angle?"

The angle is the way in which the thing can be put over with least resistance and in quickest time. It has as its target a soft spot in human nature. It has as its means a smooth working psychological vehicle that fits in perfectly with the props and equipment that must accompany it. It's a natural way of doing the thing. So, if the angle is an idea, it is most often called a "natural."

Finding the angle doesn't call for persuasiveness, for it's the angle in itself that is so persuasive it hardly needs a persuader attached to it. Finding the angle is a matter of instinct, of psychological expertness, or a fine sympathy for human values. But it has certain characteristics that act as guideposts to finding it.

First, it's *personal*. The angle is going to be about the person on whom it is to be worked. It is not only warm, human, and alive, if it is intended for John Smith, it's going to be personal—particularly for John Smith, in other words, a Smithesque angle.

Second, it's *intimate*. It's about something very private and buried deep down inside John Smith. It deals with feelings and thoughts and dreams that JOHN SMITH ONLY has experienced. If it's aimed at a large group of John Smiths, stick to the identical formula for one John Smith. For the good angle is always singular, and if it's a natural will fit a thousand men as easily as one.

Third, it's *lush*. There's a richness, a luxury, a juiciness to the angle that makes it a plum dangling before the eyes of its prey. It is never common or cheap or recognizable as anything but an original.

Every product or proposition has an angle—a basic sales or merchandising idea by which it is most easily put across to the public. Every man has an angle of his own personality that clicks instantly with all men. An honest, open, well ventilated appraisal of both the product and the man should disclose this choice "universal" which indicates the easiest road to success.

Find the angle, know the angle, use the angle!

3. REACH HOME WITH A REAL JOLT

Remember when some clumsy or unthinking friend disturbed your equilibrium by commenting too directly on your bald head, your grey hair, your wrinkles, your scars, your poorly fitting clothes?

You were upset for hours afterward—because that critic *certainly reached home.*

Now it is never wise to point out people's defects, but it is always correct to attempt to *reach home.*

Every true motive, every human, universal cause of emotional response is bound to reach home. There are certain general motives that appeal to all people, that seldom fail, that are everlastingly new, personal, and intimate—and cause prompt action. By all means learn these motives—if you don't know them already.

4. THE LARCENY MOTIVE—SOMETHING FOR NOTHING

Something for nothing! The magic word FREE!

In business, the closest experts can come to predicting in advance just what will happen involves these two merchandising schemes: The prize contest and the premium offer. People want something without having to pay for it. The more impossible it naturally is of attainment, the harder to get, the more they hope to get it. The appeal of the long shot! The desire to do the impossible without lifting a finger in work.

Almost every case in which you are appealing to a man for response and action has something free in it. Point out the free. Dwell upon the long shot. The universal larceny that's found in all men will then do the rest. Study every proposition for the basic "FREE" in it; there is always some unused leverage which can be offered without adding to expenses. "Give" people all the "free" things which they could have for the asking.

5. THE GREED MOTIVE—GRAB IT, MISTER!

Greed is pure selfishness. You could kill your brother for wearing your ties, you get mad as can be when someone appropriates that extra pencil that was hanging around your desk.

Did you ever try to clean out a desk drawer or a clothes closet and hesitate long and tenderly over parting with many a possession, which was no longer of the slightest use to you, but which you couldn't separate yourself from? What was holding you there was pure greed.

The greed motive is actuated in this simple offer: "Mister, here's something! It's a nice thing to have. It can be your permanent property! Grab it before someone else does!"

The man generally grabs, if it's offered to him strictly as a grab.

6. THE MOTIVE OF SELF-INTEREST—ME AND MINE

People don't care about you! Quit talking about yourself, quit referring to your own problems, experiences. To use those words "I" or "My," "Me," or "Mine" is just the same as saying: "Quit listening to me, this is of no consequence!"

The world is interested in itself, not you. Your great opportunity for becoming popular, remembered, desired, and helped by others is to throw your entire interest into others' lives and stop talking about yourself.

When you play to the other's interest in himself, you are covering the choicest subject within the scope of human feeling. Never spoil this heavenly delight by bringing in any reference to coarse, stupid, uninteresting you. Always remain the instrument that actuates and nourishes the other man's self-interest, and you will automatically become the motive that causes him to desire your company.

7. THE VANITY MOTIVE—EVERYBODY'S A SHOW-OFF

Everybody's a show-off. Everybody's out to prove to the world that he's a big shot. He wants to strut, to hog the stage, to tell the world of his prowess.

But the big shot isn't the one who wants to show off that bad. The big shot's the fellow who realizes the weakness of his fellow man and so piles honors, glory, acclaim, compliments on his head. The big shot continually feeds the vanity of little shots.

He seeks no honors of his own but he gets the lion's share of the honors as soon as the dust settles. He bides his time and comes away with what he wanted all along.

Let the other man show off. Don't try to knock him down. Don't point out the folly of his pride, or the hollowness of his boasting. Let him show off to you, let his hunger for importance find you as a sympathetic audience. The response you give to this terrific desire in all men's hearts will win for you their everlasting gratitude and most of the honors they themselves could never merit.

8. THE SELF-PRESERVATION MOTIVE—SAVE ME!

If you want a person to act, be sure to put up a penalty
for his non-action. He is so eager to save everything for
himself, to suffer no loss of prestige, power, of fortune
that he readily pays the price rather than suffer the
penalty.

9. THE REPRODUCTION MOTIVE
—THE PROUD DADDY

It's the other man who wants to command the action,
to bring about something new and grand, *to produce a
baby* for which he is entirely responsible and which resembles him identically. You just be the good mother
and be around when the baby is born—under no circumstances point out that you contributed anything to the
birth. All the work, worry and travail belongs to you—
resign yourself to it. The glory belongs to *him!*

Every material action of human beings—other than
the automatic physiological actions—is a formal or an
informal attempt of the human being to reproduce himself. He—or she!—wants to be a FATHER.

That's why men brag so loudly when they make a
satisfactory purchase; they're so sharp, so clever, so
strong that the product they buy becomes a reflection
of them and their ability.

In the material you offer to the man and to which you
expect him to respond, be sure you have included a
clean-cut opportunity for him to become a psychological
father!

226

10. THE CONVENIENCE MOTIVE—THE BIG LOAFER!

All men are loafers at heart; they love comfort, ease, the
short cut, the quick cure, the magic formula.

Serve up comfort. Find things for them NOT to do.
Protect them from the dust, the sweat, and the furies of
life. Don't disturb them when they're sleeping.

Let them have a taste of solid comfort, as supplied
by your deft hand and brain, and it will be impossible
to keep them away from you for life.

11. THE APPEAL TO PLEASURE—AIN'T WE GOT FUN?

At the slightest pretext the ordinary man will stop the
serious work he is doing in order to have some fun. The
desire to shed the shackles of labor and have some fun is
a dominating instinct in practically everyone. This is
why so much entertaining is going on in business today,
why conventions are so popular, why business trips are
so common. Under the perfect alibi of business, a man
gets a chance to have some fun, to be independent of
home and work for a little while. The appeal to pleasure
hardly ever misses. Some samples:

> Let me take you to lunch
> Let's hold a banquet
> Let's have a party
> I'll play you some golf
> Let's try a show, a prize fight
> Visit us in the big town

I've a tip on a horse race
Let's talk about your hobby
Let's talk about you
Have you heard this one?
It's wonderful outside
Come on for a ride
Here's something interesting to read
Can you do this trick?

12. THE BOW TO LAZINESS

Man is one great depository of laziness. Laziness is the basic reason for the improvement in our standard of living. Inventors know that anything that will save steps, motion, time, or labor will be an instant and universal success. It has been said that the patent which paid the largest number of individual royalties of any ever issued was the one covering the small rubber ball with the individual strand of rubber attached to it. Children could bat or throw the ball out and it would come back or could be pulled back without any necessary chasing or bending over to pick it up!

To ask anyone to write a postcard, or even to sign his name, is asking a great deal. If you can frame your request so that a nod of the head is enough, or even better, if you can put a proposition in such a way that if your listeners do nothing at all, they are thereby endorsing it, you are sure to go over with a bang. If you are after a man's money, never make the mistake of also asking him for his labor. Never ask for his labor in

228

any manner, shape or form, for you will not get it. The support he gives you can be either moral or financial, it can never be physical!

18. THE SELF-DEVELOPMENT MOTIVE

The only worthy motive in the bunch is the motive of self-development.

At heart we are all little children and we honestly want to grow, to make ourselves bigger, stronger, more worthy. Physical skill, education, learning and culture we seek instinctively, know we must be right if we can get it.

Feed this universal impulse in people by stimulating them to further development, urging them to grow, to work for further rewards, to bolster their courage and ambition, and never to tire till they've reached their objective.

Take the role of the inspirationalist. Go out of your way to lift a man up, to point to the higher standard, to feed the flame that hungers for success by urging him, cheering him, encouraging him. He will never forget the source of his inspiration. And if you are a sincere inspirationalist you can't fail to make something out of the man; something which may prove extremely valuable to you later on.

Arthur Brisbane was one of the most widely read writers of the world. He was an inspirationalist. The most widely read book is the Bible. It is strictly a book of inspiration. The most stirring song of every country is its national anthem—in every case it is pure inspiration.

Inspiration is so successful because it is the practical instrument that activates the motive of self-development.

14. "UNDER COVER" IS BETTER THAN "OUT IN THE OPEN"

Certain attempts at persuasion are invariably futile. A study of these failures may disclose the right ways.

Don't Teach—Inspire. You can't teach anybody anything! Don't try. Preaching is really the teaching of morality and it seldom works, too. It's too unpleasant, too harsh, too uninteresting. Nor can anyone ever be reformed, unless he voluntarily reforms himself.

There are good teachers, good preachers, good reformers, however. What kind of men are they? Invariably they are *inspirationalists.* They don't do the reforming, they inspire the subject to do his own. They teach nothing, command nothing, scold never. Their persuasiveness is ever plus, ever positive. They show their subject the light, they breathe into him courage and action, they make him believe all things are possible.

To persuade—instead of teaching—*inspire.*

Don't Reason—Play on His Emotions! Reasoning is the grand avenue to truth, but reasoning is no vehicle of persuasion. People don't know the rules of logic or of rational argument; they have no means of checking truth or detecting error. Besides, to reason with a man, to prove something to him, is to *conquer* him. He

230

doesn't want to be conquered; he wants to be the conqueror.

Man is only theoretically a *rational* animal. Actually he is all emotion, his mental ability being a faculty that tries to make his emotions seem plausible.

Don't Beg—Give Him an "Out." "Please do this for me, I've asked you a thousand times, please, please, please!" That's begging!

How often have you tried to persuade by begging and found it didn't work! Begging is annoying. Begging is cheap. Begging is unjust both to the beggar and the one being solicited. For it makes a sorry picture out of the beggar, and it puts the one being solicited into the distressing dilemma of either refusing or granting. No man has the right to limit another's freedom by tying him up with this dilemma, for whatever way he now acts will be disagreeable.

Instead of begging, *grant!* Show the person that he has the option of doing many things other than the thing you suggest.

Don't Insist—Suggest! No one likes to be bossed and a direct command often arouses a new supply of resistance in the person you are trying to sway. You have no right to be ordering people around, you have no authority that can give any substance to your command. Far better to silence the command and simply present the materials for action.

Then *suggest!*

Don't Pray—Act! No persuasion was ever affected by hoping, praying, or wishing, though perhaps those

231

means have been earnestly tried in every case. Nothing could be less practical than to think that your unspoken feelings could possibly influence the other person!

Consider! Mental telepathy hasn't yet been developed to the point where your unspoken messages can reach the one you're aiming at. Nobody's a mind reader and even if he could read your mind, he'd see nothing but selfishness there and prejudice to your own side.

Instead of that soul-stirring silent prayer, say a prayer with deeds! *Do something!* Get on the scene of action! Clean up the incompleted details. In persuasion, mind has no influence over matter, it's all "matter over mind"!

Making Up His Mind. Positive action can come from the one being persuaded only when he is allowed to make up his own mind. If he detects you are making up his mind for him, he resents your tactics and inclines to take the opposite stand.

Persuade by drawing the other man out. Ask for his opinions, his evidence, let him form his own conclusions. If he arrives at the wrong conclusion, let him; don't contradict or even correct him. What are conclusions anyway? In practically every case of anyone making up his mind, he comes to a dozen conclusions before he finds a satisfactory one. Your job is to be ready with that *right* conclusion, to insinuate it into his mind not as a conclusion, but as a simple truth, and *let him make a conclusion out of it.* Then he will be making up his own mind, and though you are his active assistant, he will insist he did it all himself.

232

15. THE INVISIBLE ART OF SUGGESTION

Suggestion is the art of getting your persuasion across to the other person without his knowing how you are doing it. You sell him—but he doesn't know he's being sold!

Suggestion addresses itself to the subconscious; it is not only invisible, it is indirect, roundabout, and apparently beside the point. But if practiced faithfully it rarely fails. And it is an art which you may easily acquire by following a few simple rules.

Throw Yourself at Him! Have you ever heard one woman say of another: "No wonder she got that man! She *threw herself* at him!" In other words, the successful husband hunter contrived continuously to be in the company or the neighborhood of the man she wanted. She sold *by being near,* she suggested by propinquity!

Propinquity is the simple suggestion of the thing being close at hand, right in front of you, easily available. The smoker draws a package of cigarettes from his pocket and passes them around. *Every man in the group takes one!* Why? Suggestion by propinquity.

If you're selling something the prospect can handle, put it into his hands. Bring it before his eyes! If it's a car or a truck or a train, let him take a ride in it. The closer his body gets to it, the closer he is to buying it.

When you're buying a suit of clothes, the fact that you try on the coat, doesn't necessarily mean you'll buy it. When the salesman suggests, "Let's see how the vest goes with that" you feel yourself slipping a little. When you finally are induced to put on the trousers, the whole ensemble, and the tailor's opinion is consulted, you know that the sale is in the bag.

Get close to your people! The closer the contact the richer the suggestion.

Tie in Your Ideas. Why so much wild struggling to prove a point? Maybe just a simple picture of the good consequences will far better serve the purpose. For the consequence suggests that an artificial proof is unnecessary. Suggestion is natural: reasoning is *artificial.*

The sturdy bodies of children in vigorous play! A big bottle of milk nearby. NO OTHER WORDS ARE NECESSARY. The consequences of good health suggest the use of milk where all the talk of calcium, lime, calories, and the like would be useless.

An old couple enjoying a winter vacation in Florida. A bank book quietly inserted in the picture. The CONSEQUENCES suggest saving.

The Build-Up. Consequences suggest what preceded; antecedents suggest what follows.

A hand setting a trap suggests there are mice in the house. A tub being filled with hot water suggests that someone is going to take a bath.

Help create the antecedent even though there is no profit in it for you. You can't sell bait unless the man has a fish pole; help him get the fish pole and the bait will take care of itself.

Get Personal. A favorable, personal report is sure to carry suggestion: "You have good color!" "You have white teeth!"

The favorable personal suggestion is *praise* handled in *the way that causes the prospect to do something more,* as "You believe in the latest," "You're a good spender!"

Aim at the Senses. Most attempts to reach the mind are ineffective. The senses, however, are right at hand, *and the senses cause the buying in the face of stern resistance from the mind.*

Your mind may decide you're going on a diet but the smell of good cooking makes a monkey out of that decision.

Sensual suggestion throws extra emphasis on physiology. One man starts scratching and pretty soon everyone in the room itches. A soft feminine voice can have just as much sex appeal as a beautiful feminine figure.

More appeal is made through the senses of sight and hearing than through taste, smell, and touch. But the latter three are every bit as potent.

Just a Whiff. A suggestion is a hint, a sample, a whiff. Never is it the WHOLE PROPOSITION! If you say to your prospect, "I want to put the complete facts before you," before you even have his interest aroused, he will be sure to reply, "I haven't time to go into that now."

You can't *prove* to another that he wants to eat a given amount of pop corn. But the smell of the freshly popping corn may start him eating at once. You may have no intention of eating a bowl of nuts, but the *taste* of one or two nuts may eventually cause you to devour a whole bowlful.

The suggestion starts slowly, mildly, innocently. But it feeds the human appetite bite by bite until the desired goal is reached.

Reminders. The church advertises: "TOMORROW'S SUNDAY." That's enough. The insurance card says "Happy Birthday." That's all. You don't have to be told you're one year older, YOU KNOW IT! And your train of thought must lead you naturally to a plan for supporting yourself and dependents sometime in the future.

To suggest by reminding, simply *remind the other of a significant fact.* A fact, several angles of which have a relation to you or your proposition, and several other angles of which indicate to him the need for quick action.

Show a Good Example! What is style and vogue? Simply suggestion by example. A number of people do the same thing; the others see it, follow the example, and there's a new style.

The use of the device of example indicates the need for initiative, for action. Simply do SOMETHING. Don't just think about it, talk about it. Do it.

Every suggestion works *the very first time* it is made. However, in most cases it doesn't work perfectly enough to cause results. But make a good suggestion *often enough* and no power on earth can stop it from bringing about the desired effect.

236

☆

The Relative Importance of Each Quality

In reviewing our list of eight indispensable qualities, and before examining in detail the relative importance of their component parts, please remember the one and only reason why the list is offered.

You are on one side of the street, and though the street is wide and the traffic dangerous, *you want to get across*. These qualities, regardless of their intrinsic value to everybody, aren't necessarily the qualities to be used in selling *things*, but rather in selling *yourself*. They are your only means of *getting yourself across*, which in the present world is the main job cut out for you. After you once learn to sell *yourself*, most of your other problems concerning material success are automatically solved.

This book cannot hand you the solution on a platter. It can only list the qualities, suggest methods of acquiring them. After being told what you need, and how to get it, your principal duty from this point on is to *practice*. Through practice, knowledge is turned into skill and ability, and becomes "second nature." Reading won't deliver to you the ability to sell yourself to others. But the right kind of practice will.

For instance, it has been shown to you that the ability to think on your feet and to speak before a group of people is an important asset. If you have never made a speech in your life, you instantly shrink from the very thought of becoming a public speaker. You are willing to try other things, perhaps, but you draw the line on public speaking.

You do not now know that though you suffer and die through your first speech, that you almost collapse in your second one, that on the third attempt you invariably begin to "feel your oats." You do not now know that PRACTICE inevitably makes the "impossible" possible. And so you regard public speaking as an "impossible" activity now. But just make three speeches and you'll like it.

Do any of the things that here have been given an important rating *three times* and you'll be surprised to learn that they are not nearly as "impossible" for you as you had supposed. Those THREE attempts are highly important, however. You can't dispense with them. You can't get anywhere without practice. And your hardest practice must be aimed at the most important things first.

Study the chart showing the detailed composition of

each of the eight major qualities. Score yourself honestly today, to learn exactly how you stand in the all important matter of having sold yourself. Consider 50 a passin, verage. Anybody who has sold himself 50 per cent may be considered as having already established himself as an *individual*.

If you honestly find you can't score 50, then start at once practicing the exercises that will give you this passing grade. If you do score 50 or better, find out the points which you have been neglecting and resolve *through practice* to acquire those abilities which will push you closer to your goal of an unusual personality, *a remarkable individual*. A score of 100!

If you must neglect or sacrifice certain qualities, don't slight the ones that represent a large number of points. Perhaps up till now you have concentrated on developing qualities which at best represent an insignificant part of the total. *Go after the high scores, important things!*

Leading the list of all necessary qualities is ENTHUSIASM which, all by itself, represents 8 points, a total as large as the whole division of Diplomacy, and larger than the divisions of Familiarity, Reliability, and Persuasiveness. Think of it! If you can acquire Enthusiasm in a rich degree, you have a quality that can outweigh even such an important quality as Reliability!

Why do we give such a high score to Enthusiasm and to other qualities such as Ability to Speak in Public and Ignorance of Others' Opinions? Simply because these qualities, though listed as sub-elements of a main division, are actually so potent, so universal, that they extend to all other divisions, creating and propagating many other qualities in their wake. For instance, no man can become a competent public speaker without automatically acquiring a considerable amount of Guts. No person can get Enthusiastic without instantly being regarded as a person dripping over with Optimism and Promise, as also being a fine example of Familiarity and Persuasiveness. And the man who has trained himself to ignore the opinions of others is bound to prove a man possessing every possible angle of Guts, as well as being a man of Spirit.

Score yourself today. Practice the exercises faithfully for a month or more. Then score yourself again and see how far, in one month, you have been able to advance yourself toward your goal.

EXPRESSION

Speaking

Speak Up 1
Speak Correctly 1
Conversation 1
Public Speaking 7

Writing

Writing Ability 2
Self-Publicity and Promotion . 5

Acting

Front	1
Presentation and Delivery . .	1
Spirit	8
Egotism	2
Enthusiasm	8

Creating

Invention	1½
Production	1½

TOTAL EXPRESSION	35	35

PROMISE

Future

Future Attitude—Vision . .	2
Plan and Program	3

Feeding Hope

Optimism	4
Plus Attitude	2

Talent

Incomplete Sampling	1
Versatility	2
Letting the Other Man Find You	1

TOTAL PROMISE	15	15

GUTS

Punch

Decisiveness	1
Aggressiveness	1

Selfishness

Purpose	1.5
Ruthlessness	.5

Ignorance

Of Physical or Moral Harm .	2
Of Others' Opinions	6

Perseverance

Sticking to It	3
TOTAL GUTS	15	15

APPROACH

Connections

Circulating Ability	1
Your Personal Build-Up . .	2
Popular People for Friends . .	2

Contacts

Asking for Interviews . . .	1
Operating Through Third Party	1
Ability to Block Refusal . .	2
TOTAL APPROACH	9	9

242

DIPLOMACY

Visible

Agreeableness	.5
Heart	.5
Humility	.5
Bribery	1.5
Patience	1

Invisible

Keeping Objective in Mind	1
Covering Up	1
Politics	2
TOTAL DIPLOMACY	**8** 8

FAMILIARITY

Sympathy

Feeling	.5
Universal Streak	1.5

Honesty

Shedding Shame	1
Simplicity	.5
Sincerity	.5

High-Keyed Make-Up

Ability to "Catch On"	2
TOTAL FAMILIARITY	**6** 6

243

RELIABILITY

Character

Truth 5
Keeping Your Promises . . .5
Health 5

Ability

Efficiency 5
Logic 2.5

Self-Confidence

Believing in Yourself 1

Conservativeness

Non-Exaggeration 5

TOTAL RELIABILITY   6   6

PERSUASIVENESS

Direct

Pressure 5
Use of Necessity 1
Use of Deadline 5

Indirect

Use of Motives 1
Playing on Weakness 5
Getting the Angle 5
Suggestion 2

TOTAL PERSUASIVENESS   6   6

TOTAL ALL QUALITIES: 100

244

☆

Do Something About It!

You may agree with every statement and principle offered in this book. You may readily admit that the "Merit System" which was drilled into you from early childhood is of practically no value till you have mastered the Knack of Selling Yourself.

But there's a real danger to all true things, especially when personal experience has made them obvious. You may admit the truth and then proceed *to do nothing about it.*

Dear reader, don't BE that way! You've read this book. You know there *is* such a thing as the Knack of Selling Yourself. How important it is. How—with serious application—it can be acquired. *Now do something about it!*

Right now the world is beckoning to you with wide open arms. The world wants—needs—more men who

245

have sold themselves, especially younger men and middle-aged men, who can be strong and important and still be able to reflect the present times.

Many of the prominent men who in days gone by sold themselves are now strangely quiet. All through the land there's a letdown in leadership, in crusading and pioneering for new things, for things that can serve the people *today*. It's because men get old, and when they get too old lose the perspective which can make them useful or important in terms of current life. The big-shots of bygone years have retained much of their power and influence but in the trials and hardships of the depression have found that many of the old formulas no longer work. So they are content to ride on past glory, and getting very little competition from younger and stronger men, maintain their uninspiring prestige unmolested.

THIS IS THE IDEAL TIME FOR YOU TO SELL YOURSELF

Take advantage of the present letdown. Competition is weaker than it ever has been before. *Do* something about it! First sell yourself—then step out and deliver something new and real to the world!

YOU'RE REALLY WORTH IT!

Before you start to sell yourself, you have to *think* about yourself! No one is as familiar with yourself as you are, and consequently out of this self-contemplation may be bred a dangerous "cheap feeling." In your own self-regard you hardly seem like much of a guy. You're inclined to belittle all your inward thoughts and feelings because they are petty, mean, and shoddy. You believe that other people are on a much higher plane than you.

You see a man who is going somewhere, or one who has already won a place in the limelight, and you call him "Leader!" "Showman!" "Master Salesman!" "Great Politician!" He's way better than mere little you, only because he has sold himself. For if you had a chance to look into his heart, you would find there the same cheap, mean fears, cares and thoughts that you yourself harbor. He strikes a pose and you think he's a big-shot. But after washing his hands he, even as you or I, leaves a dirty ring around the washstand. The buttons break off *his* shirts, and he quite frequently gets holes in *his* socks. He's really—and that means *basically* —the same kind of guy as you.

The point is, if it was worthwhile for *him* to sell himself, it's worthwhile for *you* to sell *yourself!* You have your life to lead, a family to support, and you could nicely use all of the material benefits that the Knack of Selling Yourself can bring.

Realize that you are just as smart, just as good, just as GREAT as any established "big-shot"! Don't concede that Greatness and You can never be tied together. It's just as easy for YOU to be GREAT as for any other man to be GREAT. First, *believe in yourself.* Second, plan your grand strategy thoroughly. Third, know what to do and *then do it!* There is no better prescription for success.

247

YOU'RE ONLY JUST STARTING

Years of your life may have gone by. You may have very little to show, in the way of worldly goods or of popular recognition, for the work you have already done and the time you have put in. Maybe right now you feel like calling it a day, resigning the work of the world, the special causes, ideals and undone projects you dreamed about in former years, to other and more active men. Perhaps you feel like a good long rest, with no special plans to follow up the good long rest.

Mister, please realize, you're not through—*you're only just starting!* Just yesterday, last week or last month, there was a momentary flicker of applause for something you had just done. The spark of life and love which you had put into your work lighted up, inspired, and cheered someone else. A letter was written, a word was spoken, definite recognition was awarded you.

Years ago, when you were very young and "only just starting" if you had received that much official encouragement for some action of yours, you would have turned into a wild man of ambition, your hat would have suddenly become too small for your head, you would have stepped out and bowled over the whole world in a day!

But now, caught in the thickness and stiffness of time, now WHEN YOU ARE A FULLY DEVELOPED MAN with all of your faculties trained and perfected, all of your producing equipment at the zenith of its efficiency, you are ready to embrace the foolish philosophy of "let the other

248

men have it; it's not worth the struggle!" And all because you believe your life so far has been just about
everything a complete life can be, and you're now ready
for a much deserved rest.

As a matter of fact, *you're only just starting!* If
you'll forget your AGE, forget your EXPERIENCE, forget
the PAST STRUGGLES, and just examine the present
evidence of what your work is doing to other men, how
definite your influence is on society, on industry, and on
thinking people in your special line of work, you will see
NOTHING BUT ENCOURAGEMENT on the horizon. Those
who have been affected by your words, thoughts, and
principles are not thinking about how old you are, or
how tired you are, but solely about your words,
thoughts, and principles. They find them good and acceptable.

Here in your mail box, on your telephone or your
very doorstep, is the rich, thrilling evidence of recognition you so heartily longed for some years ago when
you were "starting." What you wouldn't have given for
this happy balm then! But here it is NOW; here is what
you have always wanted, the only stuff which counts.
And *now you are ready to pass it up!*

The truth is that you weren't really "starting" then—
you were just planting, cultivating. YOU ARE ONLY JUST
STARTING NOW, and the fruits and returns of all those
labors are yours to collect THIS VERY YEAR!

So start! Turn on a little love, life and gusto. Have
faith in the ENERGY you know is within you but which
you are trying to tell yourself is missing. Regard your-

249

self as a student of world and life just receiving his
diploma after the required years of work and study,
and NOW READY TO DO SOMETHING ABOUT WORLD AND
LIFE by going out and licking them both!

Other men have decided they're through, or well
fixed, or ready to mellow and retire gracefully. But not
you—*you're only just starting* and at this time in life
when others of your age are quitting, you're only just
beginning to turn on the pressure!

MAKE A MANIFESTO!

Alive inside that brain of yours for some time there has
been brewing a *plan.* You have a plan for doing something unusual, for fixing something badly in need of
repair. You have a cause you are just about ready to
embrace, an objective you have just about decided to
reach. Inside that brain of yours, you now hold the biggest thing that has come into your life in years. The
stage is set, the ground is prepared, you know exactly
what you want to do about it—WHAT'S THE NEXT STEP?
Make a manifesto!

In the old days, when a man was on the verge of
something BIG, *he made a manifesto.* He came right out
and publicly declared what his intentions were, why he
was acting, and gave the whole world his personal
promise that he would not withdraw from his course of
action until he achieved his objective.

A noble thing—a manifesto! Kings and sovereigns,
soldiers, crusaders and apostles—great men all, invari-

ably have favored the manifesto. And they succeeded.

So why not YOU? Why don't you make a manifesto today? Why don't you come out in public and lay your heart bare? Announce to the world that the great things now boiling inside you are about to be released!

The bigger your program—the more people should hear it. You may wish to benefit humanity, to protest against a great moral wrong, to help your country through a specific danger. ANNOUNCE YOUR PLAN—SIGN YOUR DECLARATION! Or, if your motives are not quite so noble, you may only be intending to do something strictly selfish as GET A JOB BEFORE SATURDAY, BE THE NEXT MAYOR OF THIS CITY, OR MAKE A MILLION DOLLARS.

Make a manifesto! Whatever it is that's bothering you —if you can't forget, can't relinquish it, then *embrace it*—and make a manifesto!

What does a manifesto do? It puts you on the spot! As you stand now, you are undergoing an internal earthquake. You and your plan are struggling privately, and though the struggle may be ever so important, ever so deadly—no one knows about it except yourself. You can make great promises to yourself and a little later on forget them conveniently. The matter that is so vital now can easily be shelved at any time without embarrassing you, for you are the only one to account to.

But *when you make a manifesto,* you automatically tell the whole world your private business—and now you can't back out without disgracing yourself. Think! If you now make a public resolution concerning your pet cause, wouldn't the scorn, criticism, and laughter of the world force you into fighting all the harder for the things you want to see done? Wouldn't your manifesto be the MAIN MOTOR of your plan, wouldn't it get you off to a flying start, wouldn't it goad you on with unflagging courage and perseverance? Wouldn't the manifesto furnish the WHOLE ENERGY necessary to put the thing across?

Make a manifesto. Your plans, your hopes, your aims are all theoretical, visionary and impractical until you get on solid ground with a manifesto. The plan that stays *inside* too long is poison! *Bring it out!* Tell the world! Brave the ridicule of lesser men for the greater and better things in life. Make a manifesto, and if you're worth your salt, YOU WILL MAKE GOOD ON YOUR MANIFESTO!

GO INTO ACTION TODAY!

The only men who ever sold themselves were those who did all of their own self-promotion work! They didn't deputize someone else to do the immensely important job of selling them.

It would be much easier if you could find some stooge to take care of all of the mechanics of selling you. To handle the onerous details. To lick the envelope flaps. To do the footwork. To be a first-class messenger boy, a donkey worker. But nobody, even the most famous and successful example of self-promotion, has reached his status through any means other than doing most of the work himself. The big-shots have found no short-cut—and neither can you, whether you believe it or not.

The "Merit System" is all work and likewise the Knack of Selling Yourself is all work. Perhaps selling yourself is even harder work, for it requires your doing many things which are obnoxious simply because you have never asked yourself to do them before. To the man who has never appeared on a public platform, what could be more dreadsome than having to make a *speech?* What could be harder work? And unless you fully admit the necessity for acquiring the Knack of Selling Yourself won't this job be the first you will try to dodge?

You *have* to work, you *have* to exercise, you *have* to get experience in the mechanics of selling yourself. The law of practice is a natural one. If you're aiming to be an artist, you ought to be drawing all the time. If you want to be a writer, then you're writing all day and every day. If you want to sell yourself, you have to keep selling yourself every minute and every hour, in everything you do. You have to practice and practice till you catch on to the knack, till it becomes second nature with you, till finally you sell yourself unconsciously and naturally without even studying out the tactics in advance.

It's something like going on a diet to reduce. If you are a good thirty pounds overweight, you sincerely know and admit you should take off the thirty. But when you, at this stage of the game, contemplate thirty pounds as a reduction it seems so impossible, that it becomes equally impossible to take off even five pounds.

253

No improvement is ever gained in one full swoop. You have to acclimate yourself to your new campaign, firmly convince yourself you mean business, and *then go into action.* If it's a reducing diet, and you go into action, you will surely take off pounds right away. *If you keep it up,* it won't be long before you have actually taken off all you should take off.

For as you proceed, you learn; you learn the temptations that can draw you away from your high resolves and you also learn the little tricks and maneuvers that aid you in achieving your goal. As you proceed, you become an expert—whether it's in reducing or in any other campaign.

As you proceed in your campaign to sell yourself, you pick up a thousand and one ingenious devices, most of them not even mentioned in this book, that push you faster and faster into prominence. The extra skill and extra experience that come from daily study and application to this fixed goal of yours, give you the extra strength and courage that make the hardest job seem easy.

The man who has already taken off twenty-five of the contemplated thirty-pound reduction, knows that to reduce thirty pounds is a mere trifle.

The man who had already made five miscellaneous or informal public speaking appearances, knows that a formal public speech isn't nearly as impossible as it once seemed to him.

So for goodness' sake, don't say: "I'm not cut out for speech making," "I never could act as a master of

254

ceremonies," "I don't know how to write," "I might as well try to fly as write a book!" If you speak enough, you'll finally be a public speaker. If you write enough, undoubtedly some day you'll write a book. And each job will seem all too easy, *after it's done.*

The main idea is to *start. Start now!* Don't balk at any job, no matter how difficult or miserable.

Undoubtedly the best start is to *write a letter.* Write a letter to a man who has done a good piece of work. Praise him. Show him that you have caught all the fineness, the special quality of his accomplishment. You're off! Write a letter and you're away to a flying start in your campaign to sell yourself. Because if you'll write one, you'll have to write more and you'll get the fever. You'll be making a lot of valuable acquaintances by correspondence. Write a letter to a publication. The publication may print it. Now you jump right into the public eye. From a little letter to a snappy article is just a small jump. In fact, leave the "Dear Mr." and "Yours truly" off the letter and it's an article in itself!

The start is everything. So start! You'll find the going interesting, not too difficult, but fast moving beyond all your expectations. When you definitely start selling yourself, results come in so fast that often you have to turn off the machinery for a little while to allow your progress to catch up with your operations! Before you go to bed tonight make the first move—write something, sign it, and mail it to somebody!

Aftermath

☆

AN APPLE FOR THE TEACHER?

A college student objects that the knack of selling your-
self is just the same old stunt of bringing an apple to
the teacher to get a stand-in for higher marks. Selling
yourself has to be a little more skilled and subtle than
the apple trick. The student in question should not kick
at selling himself via the apple but he ought to try ways
to perfect the technique to make it less crude and even
more effective. Instead of bringing the apple, he ought
to try bringing pertinent clippings from magazines and
newspapers on the subject being taught; these clippings
being concrete evidence of his studious interest. He
might even try arguing with the teacher, where he senses
the teacher is wrong, and gain new respect for himself
thereby. He might correspond with authorities on the
subject taught and flash the correspondence on the
teacher. He might even try to evolve a new theory on
the subject being studied and challenge the teacher to
prove him wrong. He could legitimately praise his
teacher after a session in which the teacher was particu-
larly brilliant and everybody saw it. He might even be
a man, in the midst of it all, and thank the teacher after
a lecture into which the teacher had obviously put a
great deal of extra research and preparation. And, yes,
instead of the shiny red apple he could give the teacher
a much rosier, sweeter present—the gift of his perfect
attention during every minute of the class!

AUTHOR WANTS TO MAKE MILLION QUICK

A famous author, influenced by one of my chapters, dashes off an impassioned airmail letter begging me to tell him the secret of making *a million dollars quick*. Of course, I don't think he means a full million, he probably would be satisfied with fifty thousand. And even though this book has nothing directly to do with making a fortune (other than the fact that men who sell themselves nearly always end up in the money), I hasten to give the author a few items of advice. His reputation is already made, but he hasn't been able to make any money out of it. I suggest at once that he cash in on his reputation. The first way is to proceed at once with the production of a large number of stories, articles, essays, short and wieldy pieces of literature which he can submit to a large number of editors, thus invoking percentage in his favor. He can't afford to wait for an assignment; he has to start the assignments for himself. (Initiative.) Next he should purchase at least three hundred three-cent stamps. (All at one time.) He should put these stamps to work in writing fresh, practical letters to all his old contacts, editors, authors, buyers, booksellers, agents, associates, business men, fans, who know him and may be able to help him. He should write a few strong and apposite letters to several "Voice of the People" columns and get before the newspaper public. If he can start a crusade, a nice literary fight of any kind, it will help his publicity along. He should make a try for some lecture engagements as soon as possible, whether paid or not:

259

he should appear in person in certain key bookstores and spend a good deal of time with the customers. He has two things to do to make some real money in a short time: First, he must produce, in quantity and quality; second, he must promote, if not in quality, *by all means in quantity!*

NOTE ON RELIABILITY

Anything that is immature is weak, ineffective. It may be a man, a plan, a judgment, or an attitude. Immaturity is scoffed at, laughed at, treated lightly. The world knows that nothing will happen when the immature thing is presented. Since education and culture are the aims of every sober person, their possession must be accomplished, at least in degree, early in the journey through life. No personality has a chance to establish itself firmly in society until it has proven its maturity. Such maturity flows essentially from self-reliance. The craftsman passes a strict apprenticeship and after several years of serious application is regarded as a *mature* exponent of his craft. There maturity flows from training and experience. But maturity in the fuller sense is maturity of mind. The mature man is the man who has learned to rely on himself in any and every situation. He can see a prize fight or ball game and come to a definite conclusion about it without having to wait for the morning papers to know exactly what happened. And he can get so good a judgment on the situation that he can, on occasion, see where the paper has missed the point entirely. The man who learns to think for himself, soon learns to rely on himself; he sees things clearly, he remembers and thus uses experience, he acts with justice and efficiency. Maturity and culture run hand in hand, for maturity necessarily guides a man to the better things, the more important things, the beautiful things. It is too bad that in America men wait so long to mature. Too many picnics, too many radios are conspiring to keep our minds in a semi-infantile condition. The chief hope of the individual lies in his asserting himself through self-trust; in gaining his information and ability from within, not without; in acting independently of popular opinion. Through all the ages of men, bright promoters have tried to start waves of "popular culture." But there can never be any such thing as "popular culture." All culture, as all education, as all maturity, must be strictly individual. It cannot be amassed in groups nor can it be dished out as largesse. The possession of culture may be increased through educating and encouraging the individual to rely on himself, to abandon his childishness, to cut the apron strings of ready-made opinions—*to become mature!*

WRITE A BOOK

Dozens of my friends and associates in moments of bright inspiration exclaim: "I think I'll write a book upon such and such a subject!" This makes me smile.

261

*A man who never in his whole life has demonstrated he can even write a solid five-hundred-word-article talks about writing a book as he would about playing a game of golf. To have written and published a book is a wonderful asset for any man's reputation. But day dreaming and idle wishing won't get the book done—*WRITING A BOOK IS HARD WORK. *Prepare yourself for book writing by first writing a lot of letters, articles, and materials which prove you can sustain your writing over many tens of thousands of words. Walter Pitkin has given the best definition of a writer—"A writer is a man who has written a million words!" Don't say you will write a book, till you know what a book means in terms of applied writing hours; first build up your strength to the point where you know you can turn out enough words on a single subject to compose a book. Then bear down and write it—and it will remain a permanent testimonial to your energy, your stature and your character.*

THE 25 BEST SOLD "MEN"

I have been asked to put down the list of the twenty-five best sold men in history, the figures who succeeded in getting into the consciousness of the largest number of people during their time and the year that followed. Here they are in order of importance:

1. Christ
2. Shakespeare

3. Lincoln
4. Hitler
5. Luther
6. Napoleon
7. Moses
8. Julius Caesar
9. Columbus
10. Dionne Quints
11. Ghandi
12. St. Paul
13. Joan of Arc
14. Edison
15. Lenin
16. Michelangelo
17. Henry Ford
18. Churchill
19. Roosevelt
20. Lindbergh
21. Caruso
22. Paderewski
23. Judas Iscariot
24. Charlie Chaplin
25. Mayo Brothers

Notice how nearly all of these figures score high in Expression. If they are not great talkers, they are great actors and doers. All of them, too, had a flair for publicity. They saw to it that their words were published or conveyed to the masses; they knew how to keep in the public eye. Not all of them were universally popular;

263

some were more hated than loved. To none of them fame came of its own sweet will; they all had to get out and sell themselves. They had to do a lot of other things, too, but none of them was too proud, or too impractical, to stoop at the right time to do the things that made them public figures, public property. Any time you are inclined to wonder whether it's worthwhile to sell yourself, whether it's manly or phony, just take a look at this list and see if you can find here a man who was ashamed, or afraid, or too lazy to sell himself.

SOMETHING INTERESTING TO SAY

No one has any right to be considered a conversationalist unless he is either interesting or funny. Since conversation takes up so many hours a day, why not put a little zip into it? Surely no intelligent man will insist he has any right to utter a remark like, "Well, do you think we're going to have more rain?" It has been said a million times. It is as flat and useless as a parrot's "Polly wants a cracker!" Give me the man who specializes in doing his own thinking and even though his criticisms and conclusions are somewhat bizarre, I will thrill to him for I will know that here, at least, *life is going on!* And save me from that growing tribe of Woolcott disciples, the raconteurs. They may tell their stories well, but they always forget to whom they have told them; and so a dozen times, perhaps, we may have to listen to the same story *verbatim*. Give me, in place of the raconteur, the person who is funny because he's natural, who shamelessly exposes his human nature and doesn't repeat himself simply because human nature will submit to millions of such exposures without a single duplication.

GEORGE STILL DOES IT!

Years ago there used to appear in a Chicago daily newspaper a cartoon entitled "Let George Do It." While bigshots planned, bossed, posed and fourflushed, George was left to do the actual work. George was, of course, the sap in the story; on the theory that the man who does the actual work is a fall guy and a chump to let himself be taken. The "Let George Do It" era is back again, or perhaps it never went away. Somehow today you can find forty executives, leaders, and counselors for ONE George who is willing to bend his back, spit on his hands and go to work. The world is looking for a magic formula, a simple plan that will make results automatic, thereby eliminating the need for further worry or sweat. All business, social, fraternal organizations manage to run only because there are a few Georges in each outfit, sincere, capable people who work for the love of getting things done, who know that the only way to get things done is to work, *and who do not believe that talking, thinking, or wishing can ever take the place of work. It would be great if the formula-seekers, the front men and the leaders would only sample the "George" technique.*

265

A MAGAZINE READER: Does a man who learns how to sell himself acquire the Hollywood quality of *izzat*, which is described in the following clipping from *Time Magazine?*

Cinenym

Hollywood has coined and adapted words (It, Oomph) to illustrate some of its by-products, but until lately it had never found a suitable synonym for its basic commodity which is not movies, not stars, not the California sun, but a souped-up state of mind accompanied by delusions of grandeur and prestige. Such a word has now gained currency in Hollywood: IZZAT *(pronounced "iz-zat.")*

To receive several long-distance telephone calls (via lackey holding portable phone) while lunching at Hollywood's Brown Derby is to acquire IZZAT. *To work for a mere $1,000 a week after once earning $2,000 is to lose* IZZAT. *Film folk of superior* IZZAT, *putting in a phone call to an inferior, wait studiously until the inferior is on the wire before deigning to pick up the telephone receiver. Peter the Hermit, who struts along Hollywood Boulevard in his bare feet, is short on cash but long on* IZZAT.

The word IZZAT *was borrowed from the Hindus and Persians, who swiped it from the Arabic. In Arabic,* IZZAT *(freely translated) means: "the most utterly glorious magnificence."—Time.*

266

DEAR MAGAZINE READER: Undoubtedly the man who has sold himself will carry with him an amount of izzat, in greater or less degree. To be a big-shot, is to give off izzat. Anyone who sells himself is a big-shot—you can't get away from it.—J. M.

A BUSINESS WRITER: The knack of selling yourself does not depend upon merit; in fact, I think merit has very little to do with it, or even with success. From what I have observed, people are selling themselves every day in every way *but* the merit way.

It seems to me that in order to sell yourself to anyone all you need is an "act." If you are working at a moderate pace, in the "act" you exclaim: "I'm working under terrific pressure!" Thus creating upon the listener an impressive mental picture. A piece of work that is moderately good, must always be described as "brilliant, positively brilliant." If it's more than good, it becomes a "stroke of genius" or perhaps "the man is a genius, but definitely." The person who seems to sell himself best is the one who glamorizes the presentation of himself; who creates a picture of importance, false perhaps, but nevertheless *important;* who is always agreeable, dulcet-toned, and who assumes a reassuring air of "I'll never fail you, I'll never let you down" and who, having done just that, smoothly vows the same thing over again on some other contemplated project.

A sincere person is the dope who is honest enough to survey himself and his work objectively. Nothing much matters except doing a good job and doing it thoroughly. He doesn't go on a gabfest about what he's doing or about to do. He doesn't make you pay through the nose for a little something extra. He doesn't grab another guy's idea and elaborate it as his own. He doesn't expand on all the harrowing details of achieving a certain appointed end. He doesn't give you in gorgeous words the troubles he had to overcome to toss in your lap the results you wanted—he just gives you the results, without cellophane, without ribbons.

Another way to sell yourself is through the medium of publicity. This is a better way than the "act." A better way because you are not spreading the gloss yourself, you utilize a liaison agent. He is the middleman taking the punches between you and your public, dishing out the sauce that you in all modesty could never do. He creates the aura, and all you do is give a semblance of living up to it. Even your weaknesses can be built up into charming bits of human qualities. There are instances where men have employed press agents to build them up and land them in important positions or even in the movies; the popularity and fashionableness of Miami Beach is the result of constant publicity; the same thing is true of Sun Valley; the idea of John D. Rockefeller as a philanthropist was encouraged in the public mind through clever press agentry build-up around the shiny dime give-away. The vest pocket radio was introduced and pushed with a big publicity spread —movie stars, celebrities, important persons were seen or photographed with the tiny sets long before they were advertised. Ely Culbertson, bridge authority, had a bet that within one year he would make himself famous and that bridge would become the rage. He could get no one to finance his scheme, so he did it himself, almost single-handedly, through publicity—written and word of mouth—he accomplished an almost impossible feat of selling himself, and he sold the game of bridge to the extent that a person was almost ashamed to say he couldn't play it.

Today there is hardly a night club, radio star, film or music personality, company or product that does not employ a publicity man to sell them to the public. Even doughnuts utilize the medium of publicity during "National Doughnut Week"—about 200 publicity men throughout the U. S. contributing their services. Countries too are selling themselves through publicity, better known as "propaganda."

Considering the foregoing, what I am wondering is this: What choice should a careerist make—be a dope or a smart apple? Should one become an outright opportunist or should one maintain integrity and continue to live with oneself?—G. D.

DEAR BUSINESS WRITER: No one who has proven himself to be a sound worker and a cleancut producer under the merit system should ever abandon the sincerity and faithfulness that make him so valuable to the world and to the particular sphere in which he operates. Don't *abandon* your straight ability—*add* a new ability to it, the ability to sell your stuff. If, in addition to being a real producer, you can also master all the tricks for selling yourself and if you practice them to your own immediate benefit, you have no quarrel whatever with the other side of you, the side which formerly recognized only the merit system. A man of ability who can also sell himself is a much stronger entity in any sphere of human endeavor than a man who merely can sell himself and doesn't bear down in producing or delivering. The really great men in history were all men who would have scored at the top in merit; in addition, they had mastered all the pragmatic arts of achieving leadership and lasting fame.

A SCHOOLTEACHER: *What good is all my education if the world doesn't pay its just awards to the educated man?*

DEAR SCHOOLTEACHER: *I'm surprised that* YOU *should ask me that. The aim of education is not to secure the awards of the world; education is intended entirely to bring out your real self, to grow, to expand mentally, spiritually; to find the approach to contentment, happiness, to let you appreciate life and live in harmony with it. Very often the man who sells himself is not an educated man, has not the slightest idea of what education or culture means. Though he rise to the very top of the heap, he can never make up for his loss; he has to struggle to get along with himself, has to flee his own thoughts and instincts, never knows what real life is all about. The*

270

truly educated man is always the happier of the two. Yet there are far more people in the world who would like to know how to sell themselves than there are those who would like to have a real education. Their preference is undoubtedly a mistake. But as long as they feel the way they do, and as long as the world is operated on the chief basis of self-salesmanship, I am, therefore, trying to blueprint that kind of life under which the majority must survive or perish.

A COPYWRITER: Do you mean to say I should start calling my boss by his first name? Why, he'd throw me out in a second!

DEAR COPYWRITER: If your boss is much older than you—that is, fifteen years or more older, it is very difficult to call him by his first name, especially *out loud.* But it isn't so good, either, to be constantly *mistering* him, or addressing him personally with his cold dry initials. If there's too great a disparity in ages, don't try the first name stuff on him, or the initials either; but *think* his first name when you address him, and try to get along without any definite name at all. By *thinking* his first name, your voice will get more familiar, which is the next best thing to using the first name openly. As your length of service increases, as your disparity of ages grows less, as it must, study the right time to get on a first name basis with your boss. Seek to have him call you by your *first* name. A good trick in building up

271

this situation·is to sign your memos and letters with your first name only, your nickname if you wish, your name just as you would wish the boss or any other important associate to call you. And seek also to achieve the status of addressing important associates, of lesser stature than the boss, by their first names!

A PROMOTION MAN: How important is it that a man like your looks?

DEAR PROMOTION MAN: Most important! A similarity on looks between yourself and the man who can help you means that you have established a definite bond of Familiarity. You are in his same family because you look like his brother, his son, his father. People marry each other because they look alike. People unconsciously hire others and take particular likings to these certain people because of a distinct physical resemblance. It will pay every individual who is seeking opportunities in the world to build and maintain a *familiarity file,* that is clippings of photographs of people who look like your father, your brother, or if you can establish the resemblance, yourself. It is easier to know if a man resembles you, by noting the resemblance to your father or brother. Once you see a definite resemblance, arrange to see the man. When you arrive at his office you will find that his secretary looks like him also, that other employees also are in the same physiological family. You instantly feel at home in their company—you like them because they look like you. Undoubtedly the secretary will make it easy for you to see your man—the entire road to the acquaintance being built entirely on physical resemblance. It will pay you to make as big a file as you can of rich or important people whom you resemble; sooner or later, if you make it your business to meet them all, one of these resemblances will be the turning point in your fortune.

A CLERK: Under what part of your system do you classify the technique known as marrying the boss's daughter?

DEAR CLERK: This is diplomacy pure and simple—that is the final maneuver of getting the boss's daughter to say "yes." But to get her to fall for you, you have to sell yourself to her, and then the knack of selling yourself works in the same old way, namely, most important quality is Expression, next most important quality, Promise, next Guts, etc. I don't recommend that you marry the boss's daughter, even if you're good enough to sell yourself to her; rather *sell yourself to the boss* and pick your future wife by the natural emotional processes other men have followed since time began.

MORE ON LOGIC

Few groups place greater reliance on "logic" than business men. "Here's the logic of it—" is a marvelously

273

powerful prelude to a string of jumbled up facts, theories, and unjustified conclusions. It is disheartening, nay, very dangerous, to use TRUE LOGIC *on the typical business man. It cuts him to the quick, challenges his foolish mental habits, harshly exposes his ignorance. And he won't agree with it anyhow. He just can't seem to realize that logic is impersonal and universal; that the rules for drawing a proper conclusion are just as inflexible as the rules for adding up a column of figures. The business man would consider an accountant crazy if he tried to insert a new system of personal arithmetic into his bookkeeping; yet the business man fondles his own personal system of "logic" and steadfastly refuses to find out what the true laws of logic are.*

Many men, innocently and without guile, use what they THINK *is logic and make important and costly decisions on that basis, but because they don't know the mechanism they are operating fall into disastrous ways. They are the victims of "false logic" disguised as true.*

There is so much of this flimsy and cock-eyed reasoning in business, that we ought to look at a few of the standard false systems that cause so much harm and confusion.

CALLING IT LOGIC DOESN'T MAKE IT LOGIC

A very common procedure, especially in the business world, is this:

"Let's throw out all opinions and preconceived notions. Let's see what real *logic* shows!"

274

This is a very forceful preamble. It is very often successful, simply because the word *logic* is universally respected. And because so few people know the rules of logic they are ready to believe that what the other man says is logic really is logic.

But calling it logic doesn't make it logic! Don't be taken in by such glibly uttered assurances as, "You can't deny the facts!" "Here's the proof!" *Do* deny these "facts!" Do it without any hesitancy. Toss the "proof" out of the window unless it adheres strictly to the laws of logic.

The man who says it's logic, when he doesn't even know what logic is, is the greatest criminal in business. Refuse to admit a single shred of evidence he offers—he is a prize faker.

STARTING OUT WITH THE CONCLUSION

Many surveys, investigations, and research projects of big business start out with the conclusion—the thing to be proved. This activity is a travesty on the dignity of human reason. The conclusion should be at the mercy of the premises—it should never dictate what the premises are to be. But big business likes to pay for a definite conclusion and pay it does!

Perhaps in no place in the business world is there a greater opportunity for straight thinking and true logic than in research work. When the research is mechanical, technical, and its object is scientific discovery it keeps well to the road of good logic.

275

But as soon as it becomes market research, the quest of data that will determine sales and promotion activities, it goes barbaric at once. It knows what the desired conclusion is, gathers the material necessary for that conclusion only, and ignores all truths that might wipe the conclusion out.

The research agency should not be told what the desired conclusion is. In fact, it would be a mean trick but a fine exposure of false logic to give them the direct opposite of the desired conclusion just to see what would happen.

Don't start out with the conclusion. Be humble! Be open. Start out by getting the true facts, all essential evidence bearing on the subject being studied. The conclusion will take care of itself once you get the correct data. If the true conclusion doesn't favor you, see what you can do to change the things that caused such a condition. In business, as everywhere, the truth is your greatest property, and knowing the truth is your greatest advantage.

By logic you may find the truth, but never can you control the truth by logic or cause a desired kind of "truth" to present itself. The truth is *what is*. Logic doesn't make it, logic just exposes it.

PUTTING INTO YOUR MOUTH WORDS YOU NEVER SAID

The smooth operator may assume your mind will respond to anything that sounds logical and gets you to agree with his conclusion by starting you off with a premise to which you have not agreed but inasmuch as he casually states: "Now your stand on the matter is, of course,—" and with your agreement thus assumed, you are plunged headlong into a false conclusion, from which it is difficult to withdraw, without apparently contradicting yourself.

Be only responsible for what you say yourself. Don't let the other person put words into your mouth.

LAUGH IT OFF

A standard practice in avoiding a logical demonstration is to laugh it off.

You seriously set up a perfect syllogism which forces acceptance of your proof. The other man, not wanting to admit your conclusion, turns it into a joke, makes some preposterous statement only indirectly connected with the proposition and draws roars of laughter from the audience.

Your cue. After the laughter has died down. Once more repeat your proof exactly as you did at first. Never let it be laughed off.

ON WHOSE AUTHORITY?

Many a man seeks to prove a point by saying, "I saw it in the newspaper!" or, "Mr. So-and-So said so!"

Because a thing appeared in the newspaper doesn't

make it a fact. We are too prone to accept statements merely because they appear in print. The fact that they are printed has nothing to do with their truth.

Neither does Mr. So-and-So, no matter how respected or famous, *make* the truth by *endorsing* it.

Often the examples of other men or other concerns are offered as the reason why you should participate in a certain project. Such examples are absolutely unreliable, until each is examined individually and all the circumstances of the experiment are thoroughly known.

THE QUESTION!

If a subject is up for discussion, make the other person stick to it. If you have advanced a problem for him to solve, do not let him get away from the task *by talking about something else!* Nearly all examples of false logic are directly traceable to evading the question, by ignoring it; by ringing in something that sounds like it but isn't it; by making a play on words; by attacking the personal status of the questioner; by deliberately misunderstanding the question; by bringing in new and more important subjects; or by advancing personal opinions when they weren't asked for at all.

GIVING A DETAIL THE IMPORTANCE OF AN ESSENTIAL

A necessary quality in good reasoning is the ability to distinguish between the important and the unimportant.

Details are loosely said to be "important," but what is meant then is that *they simply have to be done* or the job may suffer. An essential, however, is the job itself, its whole nature, its purpose, its materials and its means of accomplishment. Details must be respected—from the standpoint of production and efficiency. But details have no place in logical reasoning.

Here's an exaggerated example of giving too much importance to detail.

Thesis: There are too many steps necessary in starting this car.

1. I have to have the key to car.
2. I have to have key to garage.
3. I have to walk to garage.
4. I have to open door of garage.
5. I have to open back door of garage to get car out.
6. I have to open door of car.
7. I have to get in car.
8. I have to put key in ignition.
9. I have to turn key.
10. I have to step on starter.
11. I have to listen to motor, etc., etc., etc.

This could go on and on! Everything mentioned is a detail. It has to be done but it hasn't any just claim to consideration with respect to the main subject. Hence the thesis goes unproved, even though the list of "reasons" is most pretentious!

279

IS ANOTHER, AND OPPOSITE, CONCLUSION POSSIBLE?

Here's a nice juicy conclusion, the man has just served up—the result of the spectacular pyrotechnics he has called "logic."

It hardly seems fair to doubt the man—because he's so sure he's right. Take his premises just as he has offered them. Now—before accepting *his* conclusion—see if you can't derive an opposite conclusion out of those self-same premises.

If such is the case—and alas! how often such really is the case!—you can throw out your fresh conclusion, the man's own conclusion, and the whole mess of "logic" of which he was so proud a minute ago.

DO YOU KNOW ANY MORE THAN YOU KNEW IN THE BEGINNING?

The purpose of logic is to find out something new.

If a long and formidable logical structure is presented to you for acceptance, subject it to this simple test:

Does it bring out anything new?

Unless it does, the whole structure is unnecessary.

COUNT THE NOSES!

The enthusiastic booster or the ordinary promoter says: "Boy, look at the crowd in that hall tonight. Must be over 500 people!"

He tells somebody else, who in turn reports the fine attendance to others. Pretty soon the 500 jumps to 800, 900, sometimes even clears the 1,000 mark.

Did you believe the first reporter? You shouldn't have done so! The thing to do is to count the noses and get the exact figures. Peek out from the wings or from the back of the hall, count the number of rows, the number of seats in a row, do a simple little multiplying and in thirty seconds you learn that instead of there being 500 people in the hall, there are exactly 119! It hardly ever fails! Oh, how figures shrink when the noses are counted.

The logical man counts—he doesn't estimate. The evidence is before you—use it. Then if you need to make a further estimate you are not so likely to go wild.

SPIRIT IS NOT PROOF

Spirit is a highly commendable thing, *but it is not proof.*

Because a man is able to vibrate like a tuning fork, slam the desk with the force of a Jack Dempsey, gesture, emphasize, and dramatize like a professional, doesn't mean that he is logical.

He sways you. But he doesn't (or shouldn't) sway your reason or influence your mind. He simply works on straight emotion—*and emotion is not proof.*

A woman's tears, for example, win many an "argument"—but they never yet won a logical argument.

A loud voice, a fiery personality, often capture the prize and cold logic goes down in defeat, but take this for consolation—truth crushed to earth shall rise again.

281

There is no substitute for logic or for logical truth.

Logic needs no loud voice, no dramatic execution, no *wallop*. Its mightiest force is its own reliability.

So when the fiery gentleman with the light in his eye starts in to give you the works, simply say to him: "Calm down, Mister. If you're trying to prove something, leave out the fireworks, lower your voice, forget the emphasis, and let's give reason a chance!"

LOGIC IS LAW—LOGIC IS NOT MAN

The laws of logic exist without the benefit of any man, hence personalities cannot enter into any logical discussion.

A thief may prove that virtue is commendable, and when he advances such proof, we must examine the *proof only,* and forget entirely that the man operating the proof acts contrary to what he is proving.

In logic no one has to come into court with clean hands. A man of disreputable character can argue just as clearly and legitimately as the respectable man. It is required equally of both that they follow the correct laws of reasoning—nothing else matters.

The disreputable character is discredited in law courts because he does not make a reliable witness, and not because he hasn't as much right to operate the laws of logic as a man with clean hands.

As soon as anyone introduces personalities into an argument, that person is violating the rules of logic. Unless the violation is immediately erased, all the beauty and fineness of logic is dissipated and no truth can result from the melee.

ABOUT ALWAYS CARRYING $50

A POLICE SERGEANT: "I never carried fifty dollars on me before except on pay day or for some special reason. Since reading your book I tried it as an experiment, always afraid that someone would try to borrow it once they knew I always had cash on me. Nobody has tried to borrow anything but a lot of my pals are now wondering whether I own a six flat on the side and am a coupon-clipping capitalist."

DEAR SARGE: Don't get nervous when people grade you up. A man who always carries fifty dollars on him sooner or later acquires the unconscious carriage of a man with money. It has to happen: If people start insisting you are richer than you are, don't contradict them. A reputation for having money is always an asset at the bank. And don't lend anybody any of that fifty. If you ever fall into the lending class, you'll never be able to keep fifty on you!—J. M.

A MAGAZINE PUBLISHER: "When I go home this weekend, I intend to give my twenty-year-old boy fifty dollars in cash. I am going to tell him: 'Keep this fifty on you for one week. At the end of the week I am going to ask you to show it to me.'"

DEAR PUBLISHER: Please get me straight: I suggest everybody should carry at least fifty, not so much to prove he is worthy of a trust, as to receive from the very presence of the money the balm, the self-assurance, the protective warmth that fifty, always on you, can give. By all means give your son the fifty. Tell him that he doesn't have to keep *that* fifty, but he always must have *fifty* on him. Get across the idea that *fifty*, not zero, is scratch. If he has a regular allowance or extra income, let him operate on that income only; if he spends some of the fifty, he should replace it at once, the idea being that he always has fifty dollars on him and he's ready to spend it if he has to. If he knows he always has to have it, he won't get rid of it. So give him the fifty, not just for a week, but forever! And feel assured you have given him a lesson in itself worth the price of a university course!—J. M.

A MULTIMILLIONAIRE: "One of the first things I can remember my father telling me is this: 'Always carry some real money on you, never go around empty!' I have followed his advice since I was a little boy. He left me a small fortune but I succeeded in multiplying it many times over. When I read your advice about always carrying fifty dollars, it sounded just like dad."

DEAR MULTI: My words may sound like your dad's, but my bank balance is a different matter altogether. Thanks for the compliment.—J. M.

A SALESMAN: "I've had a great deal of fun following your advice to always flash a bankroll. My fifteen-year-old daughter saw me peel off a roll of bills, all ones, and did her eyes almost pop out of her head! 'Why are you carrying all that money?' she asked. I told her because I had read it in your book and now she wants to meet you, wants to see what a man looks like who urges this flashing act. She thinks you're the nuts!' "

DEAR SALESMAN: Get me right. I never urge anyone to "flash" a bankroll or be ostentatious about the fifty dollars he carries. Keep it hidden, keep it quiet, give your body, your personality time to absorb it. Don't flash it or show off with it. Let the fact that you carry money be just as natural with you as the fact that you have your pants on. It is true that once at least in every day in some unguarded act of buying something or subscribing to something you will unconsciously let others know that you are a man who carries money on him. But always let it remain unconscious. To carry the money just to flash it is ridiculous. You will impress no one that way. And remember, I suggest that you carry at least fifty dollars on you, not for the purpose of making an impression, but for the purpose of giving you a little extra *guts!*—J. M.

CHANGE FOR TWENTY. *Why must the customer feel like a criminal when he hands the storekeeper or his clerk a twenty-dollar bill? Why must he submit to the wry look, the suspicious glance, the silent challenge that he is taking undue advantage of the store? Of course, he wanted to get that bill changed—he came in and purposely bought about fifty cents' worth of merchandise just because he wanted change, more than he needed the merchandise. It is true he had in his pocket just about sixty cents in change; he needed more, he wanted to break that twenty and be prepared for the morrow. Then as he hands it over he is hit smack in the face with: "Haven't you anything smaller?" or the cute psychology which doesn't take him into camp, for after all he gets the change or he doesn't, involved in the counter offer, "I'd rather have you owe me for this purchase, Mr. Smith." Or worse still, he must submit to the feeble humor of a remark like: "I'm afraid we're not in your money class, Mr. Smith!"* WHAT'S A STORE FOR, ANYHOW? TO SELL GOODS AND TO MAKE CHANGE! *With all the merchandise stocked on the shelves, why not a supporting stock of singles, fives and tens in the cash register? Can all the merchants be so dumb that they don't realize they are sending hundreds of thousands of friendly neighborhood customers over to the cold but efficient chain store* WHICH DOES MAKE CHANGE AS A MATTER OF COURSE, *and doesn't let sentiment enter into the matter? If I were a storekeeper, I'd have the biggest variety of currency in my neighborhood; when somebody handed me a twenty I'd thank him with genuine feeling for helping 'me cut down space in the cash drawer, I'd never disappoint customers whether they came in to buy goods or just crack a bill. Maybe they*

286

would take advantage of me—just about like they take advantage of the chain store (which happens to be to the chain store's advantage). And perhaps they would even reach the delusion that I was successful and making money, just because I had loose change around. Which impression, I wouldn't object to at all, if I were a storekeeper.

DEAR JIM: I hear you have written a book called *The Knack of Selling Yourself.* This is a peach of a title and a book of that kind, written as only you can write it, ought to do a world of good. How about making me a present of an autographed copy?—Old College Chum.

DEAR OLD COLLEGE CHUM: You, like a thousand other intimate friends and close acquaintances, must imagine that I own a room somewhere, a great big spacious room with a very high ceiling, and that in this room I have stacked up copies of my book all ready to pass out as souvenirs. Since you have now reached a mature age, please be advised as to how the publishing world is run. The publisher prints and binds the books; the author does not. If the author has any books to give away he had to procure them by the same process that any honest or sincere reader procures them; he *bought* them. Surely you would not ask me for what the book cost me in cold cash? That would be begging! *But what is the difference?*

Please be advised also that the test of sincerity is

money laid on the line. If you part with the necessary legal tender to secure a copy of my book, the chances are you will try to cash in on your investment by reading the book, whereas if you got it for nothing, you might ignore it. And another consideration, this a very human one. Since I truly am an old college chum of yours, and since the time was when we were deeply interested in each other, why haven't you shown a continuance of this interest by buying a copy of the book sooner? Surely writing a book is no easy job. Surely, after a quarter century has rolled by, you ought to be interested in how an old college chum's mind works as only a book can disclose it. I'll tell you what—*you write a book,* or tell me of any of our mutual chums who write a book, and I'll put in a standing order for the first copy in every case. What I'm hinting is this: The qualities you need to brush up on are Diplomacy (Are You Too Cheap?) and Familiarity (What Kind of Buddy Are You?). And please excuse the very evident lack of Diplomacy on my part in writing you so frankly.—Author.

DEAR AUTHOR: *I meet my boss at the station. There is no red cap in sight. He has only one bag. Should I offer to carry it?—Branch Manager.*

DEAR BRANCH MANAGER: *Make your choice once and for all between being a servant, a shoeshiner, a waterboy, and a real man. If the boss has two bags, you ought to help with one—that's sharing the load. If he has only*

288

*one, and you carry it—you immediately confess to him
and to the world that you are a flunky at heart. Of
course, if you were to follow the rules of Diplomacy
only, it would be far better to carry the bag—that's
service. If the man were not your boss, but rather a customer or a friend, it would be service pure and simple,
and greatly appreciated by all. But since the man is your
superior, the situation changes entirely. Carry the bag
and you're a flunky in your own and in his eyes, too.
Refuse to carry it, and you run the risk of his thinking
you an ignorant upstart. Make your choice between
Diplomacy and Expression—which quality do I say is
more important? Expression, of course. Choose Expression over Diplomacy and* LET HIM CARRY HIS OWN BAG.
*You may offend him, but at least you will establish
yourself as independent and nervy. It's worth the risk.
And risk or not, sell yourself or not,* NEVER BE FLUNKY
FOR ANYBODY!*—J. T. M.*

DEAR AUTHOR: The doctrine you preach in your book
sounds very much like bunkshooting and bullthrowing.
Do I have to be a bullthrower to sell myself?—Auditor.

DEAR AUDITOR: I'm afraid I have to admit that every
man who sells himself has to be somewhat of a bullthrower. Not a bullthrower in the sense of the person
who goes around all day long in a loud voice telling lies,
making horrible exaggerations, loosely flinging words,
sentences, and statements just to hear the sound of his

289

own voice. But bullthrower in the sense that he has a VOICE, that he uses it generously and without reluctance, and gets his opinions across forcibly and decisively. You don't tell lies, and make ridiculously exaggerated statements. The "bull" you throw is the truth. And you throw it in such a way that you make it stick! —J. T. M.

DEAR MR. MANGAN: I only send out fifty cards at Christmas, though I could enlarge the list and send out two hundred. Is it worth while to send cards to the larger list?—Lawyer.

DEAR LAWYER: By all means enlarge your list and send a card to everyone whom you can theoretically justify as a Christmas card receiver. Christmas comes only once a year; a card is a letter of greeting one sends to a friend at this special time. No one writes as many letters during the year as he should; Christmas is a great opportunity to make up for this failure. Every card you send will create a soft spot in someone's heart for you. Send out all you can! As a lawyer, this gives you the chance to advertise ethically.—J. T. M.

QUESTION: "I have found an easy way to answer letters. I write, in pencil, a brief answer in the margin next to where the question is asked and send the original letter back. This requires no stenographer, no dictation, and is very handy. Do you approve?"

ANSWER: "No, I do not approve! To send an original letter back to anybody is an insult. Everybody takes pride in a letter he has written; when you send it back it tells him the letter was worthless, it has no right to existence, in fact, its existence is now over! You are not being smart in scribbling on letters and returning them. You are simply advertising to people that you are a lazy, insulting slob!"

QUESTION: *"I make $50 a week. How much should I pay for a suit?"*

ANSWER: *"Regardless of whether you are married or not, and regardless of how many other expenses you have, when the time comes to buy a suit, a man who makes $50 a week ought to pay at least $75 for the suit. It is true that most $50-a-week men pay anywhere from $50 down to $25 for their suits, and the suits identify them and their limit to the world. Go above your limit and pay $75. If you are easy on clothes, the $75 suit will last you so much longer it will justify the investment economically. If you are hard on clothes, pay the $75 and look good for once in your life; a cheap suit is an abomination on a man who is hard on clothes!"*

QUESTION: "Do I have to be big physically to sell myself?"

ANSWER: "No, just look at the list of the best sold men in history, and you'll find plenty of small men high on the list. All things being equal, it is true that a big body is an asset for any salesman. But small and medium sized men who are out to sell themselves make up for their lack of size with an excess of spirit. Master the science of selling yourself and forget your size!"

QUESTION: "Are showmanship and the Knack of Selling Yourself the same thing?"

ANSWER: "No. Showmanship is a form of expression only (Speaking, Writing, Acting, Creating). It is true that a good showman invariably sells himself, because Expression rates so high as a quality. And any man can sell himself, without the use of showmanship. It's all a question of what quality you decide to specialize on.

QUESTION: For purposes of selling myself would it be better if I wrote a popular song hit or a book?

ANSWER: There are somewhere between 3,000,000 and 5,000,000 people in America trying to write song hits. Just a handful of songs, out of the millions attempted, ever reach the classification of "hit." And of the people who write the undisputed hits only a small percentage become known to the public at large.

There are about 10,000 books published in the United States in any given year, and probably five times as many are written as are finally published. In bookwriting your competition is less, though the work may be harder; still if you write a good book, sooner or later it will receive proper acclaim, and finally win on its merits. You could write a thousand good songs in your life, and every song be good enough to be a hit, and yet none of them might ever see the light of day if you didn't "know the ropes" in song plugging and promoting.

Since what you want to do is sell yourself, and the question refers to which medium, I'd say by all means choose bookwriting over songwriting. If you should write a song and be lucky enough to make it into a big hit, your friends, your acquaintances and your public most likely will become irrationally jealous of you and your good fortune; everyone will think you have made a million dollars out of the song long before you have ever collected a penny, and all of them will ask you every time they meet you exactly how much you have made, when you're going to write another, what kind of a pull did you use, etc. (I speak from experience.) Write a book and the whole world will look up to you, respect you, and nobody bother about how much profit it yields you, even though it makes many times as much money for you as the song.

QUESTION: I am an aspiring writer but have no hope of ever having my writing accepted. What kind of writing is most likely to gain acceptance?

ANSWER: That's easy. There is one kind of writing no

editor can blue pencil, no publisher return. It is sure to please, sure to satisfy. As soon as you complete this kind of written document and make one or two other simple moves, it is bound to be accepted. In fact, the acceptance is *guaranteed by Uncle Sam.* Of course, I'm referring to the writing of *letters.* All you who have had hundreds of returned manuscripts bounce back on you, console yourself with this solid thought; every personal letter you write clicks! It gets there. It does the job. It never comes back except in the form of an answer. When particularly downhearted at receiving too many returned manuscripts, try writing a few personal letters to friends or relatives in a distant city—notice the feeling of relief you have as you mail them—*you just know they won't be rejected.* Write *enough* personal letters and you soon become conscious of *being the manufacturer of a great volume of acceptable writing.* The professional confidence resulting from a large quantity of such correspondence helps give your other writing the *acceptable* touch.

QUESTION: Should I keep my desk clean or all cluttered up with papers?

ANSWER BY DREIER: "We watched an executive pawing over papers on his desk to find one he had tossed into the mess a day or so before. He wasted his own time and the time of his visitor.

"The place for any paper not in active use is in a

proper file. A man who gets a great deal of work done without apparent strain is a clean desk advocate. Every paper on his desk is a challenge to him. He is far more interested in getting papers off his desk than he ever is in getting a golf ball into a hole.

"He carries the golf idea into his business. Just as in golf it is his purpose to get the ball from the tee to the hole in the green in the fewest possible number of strokes, so in business he tries to get desired results with the fewest possible motions. A paper that is handled over and over again is taking part in a time and energy wasting operation.

"A house that is cluttered with things tells the visitor that it is managed by a bad housekeeper. A cluttered desk is evidence of the same kind of inefficiency.

"A cluttered desk is an advertisement of a cluttered mind."—*The Curtis Courier.*

ANSWER BY MANGAN: If you are an executive purely, keep the top of your desk as clean as a whistle. If you are a creative man you are privileged to have it all cluttered up at all times. Such a jumbled condition suggests the creative process and serves to advertise your type of work. No creative man should make the mistake of keeping his desk clean and clear.

TIP ON SHOWMANSHIP

Most people who are able to sell themselves possess what is generally known as "showmanship." Showman-

ship is the ability to call the attention of the whole populace to your particular performance. Its chief good is
that it multiplies the effect of your salesmanship; instead
of swaying one or a dozen, you move thousands, tens of
thousands, millions your way.

Showmanship is the ability to sway the many. It calls
for a fundamental knowledge of the appeals that move
people. But even before its use of psychology it demands a mastery of an even higher ability—the ability
to act. Every showman is at heart an actor, eager to
strut across the stage of life, to capture his enormous
audience, to hold its attention and to win its applause.

You have to act to be a showman. To act you have
to be able to appear to be something you are not, to
assume a character and a role that is not now your own,
yet in acting it, it becomes your own, natural, intense,
spirited.

As a showman you act, not to a small, special
audience, but to the whole wide world; your appeal must
have universality, your role must be understandable by
the millions, and your acting rather than be merely
natural and simple, must be irregular, sensational, exaggerated, monstrous, superlative, unique and record
breaking. Your role must be dictated by originality and
your performance of the role must be superhuman. And
all the while you must follow *every rule of the actor
craft,* for without good acting there can be no showmanship!

We are inclined to think of showmen as born phenom-
enons. Actually the showman is no different from any

other actor. His audience is a little different, a little more important, that's all. If you have originality and spirit, and obey the prime law of the stage which is *practice,* you can surely be a showman. There is no trick or gift to it. Try it often enough, practice it long enough, train yourself faithfully and fully for the actor's role and you can't fail. That's the very ordinary system for becoming the most extraordinary of men.

BEFORE PERSUADING—STUDY YOUR MAN!

In the first instant you have a meeting with a new person, your mind automatically flashes this question to yourself: "What is he like?" Then your powers of observation, aided by your ready emotions, go to work. In a split second you take in his size, his complexion, the size and shape of his features, any peculiarity or abnormality which shows externally. You realize that it is important that you get a line on his personality instantly, for this quick diagnosis must be your guide to how you seek to influence him, reason with him, and handle him. There are in general four systems of study to guide you.

1. *The Feature System.* This system suggests that any man's character is readable and visible in his features and his external movements. Judge the features (a) by size and (b) by shape and (c) by special action.

Eyes: Large, round eyes suggest a sincere trusting

297

character, especially if the gaze is steady, direct and unafraid. Small slanting eyes indicate inward plotting or scheming and questionable truthfulness. Bulging eyes bespeak pronounced selfishness. And the person who won't look you in the eye at all tells you out loud he or she is shifty in character. (Caution.) But every one of these rules about eyes may be upset by the next person you meet!

Head: A low brow suggests the low brow and the high brow, the high brow. Yet the score set up by the brow may have to be changed by the size and shape of the rest of the head. A lot of distance from the ear to the crown of the head indicates undoubted brain power and intellect. When high mentality is present, too, it almost invariably reflects itself in the face and especially the eyes of its possessor. A long head and face show thinking propensities; a short face, impulsiveness.

Nose: A big nose means unselfishness, unless it is distinctly the "beak" type which bespeaks predatory tendencies. A big nose, whether unselfish or acquisitive, is also a good indication of curiosity. The big nose also advertises the person as being direct, pointed toward something definite and on his way to get it!

Lips: Thin small lips are said to indicate cruelty, firmness, rationality. Full large lips reveal a highly emotional nature, well developed sensual appetites, and a love of comfort and ease.

Chin: A strong chin that "sticks out a mile" indicates

first-stage courage, aggressiveness—though this courage may not continue through bitter strife to the end. A receding chin, or a "weak chin" as it is most often called, usually proves first-stage weakness, though it may conceal an amazing amount of lasting hardness and courage when the going gets really tough. A large heavy chin and jaw usually proclaims a stolid, slow moving, stubborn nature.

No feature can be taken as an infallible guide to character. Observation of the features, however, helps you to come to some theory quickly, and once you establish your theory, from that point on, you can amplify and substantiate it by further evidence, especially such evidence as the features display when they go into action. Do the eyes light up? Do the face muscles go into play with speech, with laughter? Do the acting features frighten, disgust, or attract? Are gestures, mannerisms, accidentals, natural or mistimes; awkward, affected?

The intellectual person must be reasoned with. The selfish, lazy, sensual person must be influenced by appeals to appetites, to comfort, to labor saving and general pleasure. The selfish, predatory type must be shown the definite profit, the percentage in his favor.

2. *The Resemblance System*. This system of character determination is based on the feature system but is a much easier one to practice.

You simply liken your subject to someone you already know, a person whose character you know through previous association. Each new face and body you see will remind you, if you train yourself to seek the association, of some person whom you have already categorized. "Whom does he look like among all the people I've ever known?" is the question. A quick search of your memory may bring back to your mind a man whom you haven't seen or heard from in years, but whose character was proven, to you, not merely by the reading of his features, but by the test of time and experience.

This is the great advantage of the Resemblance System. If features mean anything, they have proven their meaning in experience. Character was revealed by actions and results. Now the new person has the same features, and instead of going through the trouble of synthetically building his character, you are able to theorize that he must be like the characters that had the same kind of features as he.

Either the features furnish information or they do not. If they do, then use your past experience with those features as evidence of just what traits of character they divulge. If this man you are now analyzing looks like someone you have known, then he *must* be *like* that very person, at least in the qualities connected with the same features!

The Resemblance System requires a good memory for faces and people—so that you do not have to wait long minutes or hours to find the familiar one who is resembled by the new one. The best way to develop the memory is to practice the system of resembling every new face to an old face; practice it at every opportunity. Even if you are not meeting or seeing many new people, you can find photographs everywhere—in newspapers and magazines. *As fast as possible,* on seeing the photograph try to resemble the person shown in the picture to a definite person you already know.

3. *The Aura System.* Every human being throws off in a greater or less degree, a semi-spiritual radiance, called aura. *Aura can be felt,* and definitely, though it is invisible! This aura is partly physiological and partly psychic, part of the body and part of the mind. You see it proven every day, especially in cases of "dynamic personalities."

A man walks into the room, and you *feel* his presence, even before you see him physically. His "personality aura" makes itself felt before his actual person works on you physically. This aura is his *life force,* his mentality, his spirit, his body chemistry all combined. Even though it is unweighable in terms of grams or grains, it is still there. You see it when it is there richly; train yourself to find it even in a minor degree.

For the aura given off by a person is a cue to his character and to the proper way of handling him. You can actually *feel* whether he is friendly or stiff, warm or cold, logical or emotional.

Find the aura by taking a few seconds off from your analyzing, your planning, your theorizing. *Just go blank*—as if you were a piece of litmus paper. Let the other work on you. Then come to, see whether you're blue or pink; *your* color will reflect the *color* of *his* personality.

4. *The Mind-Appraisal System*. This system ignores features, resemblance, and aura. It relies entirely on the subject revealing his character in his words and deeds.

Words are labels of ideas, and ideas are the direct progeny of the mind. These ideas are either false, affected and unnatural, or they are sincere and truthful.

If your subject is throwing false and insincere ideas at you, he must have a reason for so doing. Certainly it is not difficult, if you really make a study of it, to detect insincerity and affectation in another's words and thoughts. The whole trick is *don't believe too readily*. The man may be sincere and genuine, yet no harm will be done by your letting all of his sincere expressions pass unbelieved for awhile. The time will soon come, if he is sincere, when you will naturally swing over to him, satisfied that you now know him through and through. Don't rush into it!

On the other hand, if the person you are studying is an expert deceiver (and many people have practiced the art so long that they often deceive themselves into believing they have a character which they do not at all possess), it will pay you to let the flood of his insincerity and falseness pass, till in an unguarded phrase, word or gesture he reveals his true self. Wait for *his first inconsistency*. Pounce on it. Being opposite to his previous stream of phony talk, it will disclose a basis for his true character. From this point on, no matter how false or deceiving he is, you have something with which to compare all his utterances. And he will thus tell you all about himself, even though he is telling lies.

The genuine person, on the other hand, always remains consistent in his genuineness. Not having practiced the arts of deception, it is hard for him to become affected or insincere. Thus, from the very absence of all inconsistency, you are enable to accept all his information directly and at its full value. It is not difficult to understand such a person.

The character of a person's words also discloses many definite facts about his ability. If his words are in a jumble, you can know his mind is in a jumble. And he is hardly entitled to be considered a "big shot" by you. If he has a slipshod mind, you can be sure he will be slipshod in many other characteristics. But if he speaks with intelligence, you can know he is orderly in his actions and being possessed of thinking ability should be adept in his particular trade or profession. There never was a man of intelligence and skill who was a silly or a sloppy talker.

Here's the real key to anyone's personality: *Listen.* Listen when he speaks, listen as if you were one of a thousand sitting in a public hall while he made a speech. In such a situation, you would pay keen attention, you would weigh every word, you would criticize defects, you would look for the motive, you would mentally "shoot holes" in his logic. Criticize the same way now, though you are the only one in the audience. Give him and his words your complete attention and in a few minutes he will divulge a clean-cut pattern of his inner character, his pet ideas, hobbies, and most important of all, his weaknesses.

DEFINITION OF "A REGULAR FELLOW"

DEAR JIM: I'm sorry but I just can't agree with your ideas about "selling" yourself. I think they're *all wet to the saturation point.*

If a man did the things you suggest I'm afraid he'd be a loud-mouthed, blabbering "show off"—the kind of a guy you'd want to throw things at; he'd probably be so self-centered he wouldn't listen to your opinion on *any* subject; he'd be a "floor hog" and an exhibitionist —the kind of a .... that tries to do all the talking; he'd be just another lapel tugger and back slapper with a "false face" smile—in short a pain in the neck.

I think the guy that gets along is a friendly, sincere sort of cuss that isn't too modest or too bold either; he says what he means; he'd buy you a drink even if he knew you didn't have the dough to buy him one; he works hard and does his damndest to do a good job—a regular fellow.

You'd like a man that has the qualities I admire—the hell of it is there are too few of them. Sincerely, M.C.B.

SUNDAY SCHOOL SERMON

DEAR JIM: *The thing is, Jim, I just don't like the point of view you express in this book. It may be true that successful people have to use the stratagems which you expound. Maybe most of them use these wiles unconsciously. Maybe only a few of them do so consciously.*

But my feeling about these devices is well summarized in the quatrain you find in some of our better taverns, paraphrased as follows:

> *"I do not like them, Dr. Fell,*
> *The reason why I cannot tell,*
> *But this I know, and know full well,*
> *I do not like them, Dr. Fell."*

Jim, year in and year out, I see a great many business men. Some of them have ability and use these stratagems you suggest to sell that ability. And I find I invariably shy away from them. If they were not able, I should certainly give orders to the Purchasing Department never to do business with them again. I have also met men who toot their own horns in this way and who have no ability. I just can't wait till they leave the office, and when they ring up on the telephone, I am in conference.

All this is pretty straight from the shoulder, because I know you want it that way. I myself want to be candid, since I feel even more strongly than I did when I wrote you last time about this. The times are such that we need Quality No. 3 and Quality No. 7 much, much more than any of the others you list on page 30. We don't want to make a race of Americans who don't let a single day pass without engineering at least one formal piece of publicity in their own behalf. We want men and women with the old-fashioned virtues of steadfastness, intelligence, ability and character. Now that my little Sunday School sermon has ended, please forgive me. Cordially yours, R. S.

MR. JAMES T. MANGAN: *To be able to have written this you knew human nature. People are naturally good. God created man that way. If that good can be awakened it will express itself. I believe deep down in every man's heart he has that desire to make his fellow man happier.*

He may not know how to go about it. Anyhow many of us who think and claim that we do know the right way are trying to help Him and give Him all the light we have thereby using that as a means of gathering unto ourselves more light. That is, are we burying our talents or are we putting them to use?

I do sincerely want to say to you, dear Mangan, whenever you have that impulse or urge to write or say something good, don't put it down, let it speak. To me that is God speaking through man. Of course you will never know how much good has come of this one article. So "Onward" is the word. Sincerely yours, T. G.

DEAR MR. MANGAN: A year or so ago I parted with the necessary shekels and bought your book, *The Knack of Selling Yourself.* At that time I would have seriously doubted whether anyone could reduce personal success to a set of rules.

Far from "reaching the other side of the street" as you put it, I'm just started. But here are a few of the stoplights I've passed during the last year:

Six speeches on subjects ranging from the buying of artwork to "How to Get a Job."

306

Two radio talks.

Sponsored a series of classes on Graphic Arts selling.

Worked on the Publicity Committee for the local Junior Chamber of Commerce.

Wrote (and had published) four trade paper stories.

Served on the Board of Directors of the Portland Advertising Federation, took on the direction of programs and the complete writing of a house organ.

Made dozens of new, important contacts (not the full 100, but close to it).

Had four offers of good jobs, two of these in selling, two in advertising.

Increased my earnings over 20 per cent.

All this from a guy who two years ago was a fairly good layout man, but a knee-knocker in the presence of more than three people.

All this by way of thanking you for the best kind of help one man ever gave another. I'm sold!

And this letter . . . a couple of weeks ago . . . Harry Collins, from whom I buy a set of plates now and then, ran a famous piece of your copy and reminded me that I ought to write to you. Sincerely yours, B. D.

DEAR MR. MANGAN: Here's one for the "Believe It or Not!" column:

I started to read *The Knack of Selling Yourself* at nine o'clock last night.

I laid your book down at five-thirty this morning!

And, instead of being exhausted I am much more refreshed than had I slept the night through.

I found myself quarreling with some of your points. on first reading but on rereading you had me thoroughly licked and on the third reading I wore out two blue pencils with underlines to emphasize points which I want to reread daily until good habits have replaced bad ones.

When you can get around to it, this is a formal request for you to write another book in similar vein on the knack of selling yourself through other people or the not-so-gentle art of sales management.

My very sincere compliments to you on a most inspiring work. Cordially yours, E. V.

DEAR JIM MANGAN: I am enclosing my check for which please send me an autographed copy of your book, *The Knack of Selling Yourself*. Be sure it is autographed as one of my hobbies is collecting autographed books where I know the author. You may not think I know you. However, I am a member of the Dartnell family as you are. That automatically makes us acquainted.

I want to enter my order right now for every book that you ever write, provided that you do not write one that will cost several hundred dollars per copy. Also, I want to enter a stop order in case of my death.

You get a zing into your writing that I wish I had. Sincerely yours, J. A. M.

ADDITIONAL THOUGHTS ON PUBLIC SPEAKING

A man writes me saying his wife is a professional book reviewer and has given over one hundred lectures in two years. He is proud of his wife but very uncomfortable because she is such a good speaker and he has never made a speech in his life. How is he to learn? Or should he give up and let his wife be the public big shot of his family?

I told this man no, he should not give up and no matter how talented and eloquent his wife, his duty to himself and to her was to be an even bigger big shot than she is. I told him to observe the case of his wife, how long she has been at the public speaking, the things she went through to learn it, and suggested that was exactly the way he must master the art. After he had made a hundred speeches in public he would be every bit as good, and possibly a much better speaker, than his wife.

The man made one remark in his letter which I consider worthy of further discussion. In describing the terrors of a few brief appearances he has made in public, and the agony of even having to *think* of making a long speech sometime, he said: "Of course, I don't suppose the actual conditions surrounding a speech will ever be as bad as I now imagine them."

I had to disillusion this would-be speaker, and tell him

that was where he was dead wrong. No matter how unfavorable the conditions you imagine will surround your appearance in public, know this for sure, the actual experience will be even worse. Generally when we dread the worst, actual reality turns out not nearly so bad. Not so in public speaking!

When you get up to make a speech, whether you are the veteran of five hundred public appearances or this is your maiden effort, the breaks are going to be entirely against you and the only breaks you'll get are those you make for yourself! It never fails. Wild as your imagination has been in creating things to fear about your speech, the actual event will develop even bigger fears and greater dangers just as you are about to start. Prepare for the worst—it is bound to happen!

Most of the troubles surrounding your appearance will be due to the faults and slips of the managers of the event. If you have been expecting to speak in a nice rectangular shaped hall, off an elevated platform placed at one of the long ends, undoubtedly the management will have prepared a spot for you directly in the middle of the hall, with your audience split neatly in two, nobody in front of you, half the listeners on your right and half on your left! If you think it's easy for the most accomplished speakers to operate in a place like that, you're crazy. It's going to be twice as tough for you, as you give one side of the room alternating sentences from your speech.

Of course, you are hoping for a nice introduction from the chairman. Well, keep on hoping! If it is at all possible, and it's indeed highly probable, for this man to spoil your speech, he will gleefully do it. If your name is easily mispronounced, have no fears, he will mangle it beyond recognition. He will no doubt change your middle initial. He will try to recite some high points from your life, but this material will be alarmingly skimpy and you will wonder if your life has been as empty as all that. He will probably try to tell a little funny story about you, end up by making you as ridiculous as a Chinaman, or a monkey, or a cockroach. Then he will give the audience the title of your speech, some subject altogether different from what you plan to speak on. With that, and a smulking smile of victory, he sits down and you stand up!

When people invite you to talk, they should cooperate, but they seldom do! The last speech I made was before an organization that had asked me to talk six times over a period of three years before I accepted. They had flooded me with letters, phone calls, political pressure. I finally gave in. After *accepting,* up till eleven o'clock on the day on which I was to make the twelve o'clock speech, I didn't even know *where* the speech was to be given. I was promised notices but to date have received none. I felt as if I was a stranger at my own crucifixion! And this treatment from a bunch that up until the sale were turning the world upside to get me to talk.

I have several times been inveigled into donating a week's preparation and research into a worth-while message, and have come to the banquet hall girded to give the speech of my life, figuring that all the work was justified because of the attention my message would get, only to find *I was going to share the evening's spotlight with one or two other prominent speakers!*

I remember the night I was to give the speech of the evening to an important group of a thousand sales executives. When I arrived the hall was dark, and at first I thought the affair had been called off or I had made a mistake in dates. Nothing of the kind. A movie show was going on. A rip-roaring rollicking movie, clever and funny beyond words, regaled my audience with a super-professional performance as a warm-up to my sound but not-on-film entertainment! After allowing my heart to sink all the way to the basement as I watched the swell show, knowing how hard it would be to satisfy that already pleased audience, I got so mad at the program chairman that when my time came, I went up there and made them forget they ever saw a movie in their whole lives!

Just as I was starting a speech once, a man in the audience threw a fit. It took about five minutes to get him off the floor. Another time half the audience walked out, just as I was introduced. I refused to get up, telling the chairman to keep up a running line of patter. It was a factional difference in the association and after some patient shuffling, the audience came back. They should have been tough but they were really great to talk to after that argument. I can honestly say I have never felt the pang of pain that any speaker must feel when individuals walk out on him while he is speaking, but I do know it happens about once out of three times, and *that* is something for a new speaker to worry about if he cares to!

No, you're not able to dream of all the bad breaks you can get. Maybe you'll be asked to start talking while the waiters are still serving, while the dishes are still clinking. Pericles himself couldn't do a decent job under such circumstances, but it happens every day! I once had a program chairman try to strap a small microphone on my chest just before my speech, making me look like a deaf mute or a telephone operator. "You're not going to put that thing on me!" I told him. "Oh yes I am!" he replied with great assurance. There was a brief tussle up there at the speakers' table for a few seconds, but I won. He didn't strap the darn thing on me!

If you try to use the mike, there may be an amateur engineer somewhere in the hall who is giving your voice ups and downs, squeaks and squalls, making you an alternate weakling and a roaring beast. Or the main doors may be left open and a bunch of yokels crowd in at the doorway peering at you in much the same way they do at the animals in the zoo. Or loud music may be playing in the next room; or with the full approval of the chairman, a drunk in the audience may be making funny remarks and have half your audience roaring at him and ignoring you. In such a case, if the chairman won't help you by quieting the audience, make your speech short and snappy—you can never compete with a funny drunk. If the heckler is sober, it's a different matter, give him a fight, and use the superior weight of

313

your position to properly flatten him. No audience, and no chairman, should ever allow hecklers to interfere with a speaker—but it happens, yes it happens.

The worst speaking layout I ever had to contend with was a large hall seating 500 people. The hall would have been ideal for a surgical clinic bcause the stage was way down in the bottom of a bowl and the seats towered in rows above and around the speaker. Such an arrangement is ideal for the audience which loves to be comfortable and to dominate the speaker from the surrounding heights. But the poor victim on the stage—what of him? It's an inviolable rule that the speaker should always speak from a level above the level of the audience thus giving him the physical and spiritual domination that helps him give a better speech. But in this particular hall, domination is the last thing he can hope for. The place was full, and I felt I was in good form as I started, but couldn't feel the audience; they were cold as could be. I didn't know what was the matter till I had gone on for twenty minutes without even a ripple of reaction. On sensing the unevenness of the combat, and again getting mad at the architect who laid out that hall, and at the directors who stupidly would sacrifice any speaker who spoke there, I worked myself up into a lather, stuck on the stage a half hour longer than I had planned and ended up where I should have been at the start—with the audience down in the hole and me up on the eminence!

These are just a few of the troubles a public speaker faces; most of them due to the stupidity of the arrangers of the meeting, and most of them inescapable. I hope my friend, the would-be speaker, on the evening of his first formal attempt at speech-making doesn't meet with the fate once met by a friend of mine, an accomplished speaker who has thrilled hundreds of audiences. He had been invited by a respectable group of colored people to speak at a colored church on a given evening. The cause was one of great civic interest—in fact, the very homes of the people in question were at stake. My friend arrived at the "meeting" on time and was met by the parson who, ringing his hands, lamented that not one of the many hundreds expected and promised had put in an appearance! After a half hour's waiting the speech was called off, on account of *no audience!*

PROMISE NEVER SUBMITS TO A SHOWDOWN

The person with promise never submits to a showdown. He never allows himself to accept a challenge, to engage in a competition, to be measured by a test, that may result in a cleancut decision concerning his ability.

Promise is strictly ability "that is going to be delivered." It concerns only the good things, the feats and accomplishments that are "going" to come. Of its very nature it is boundless and immeasurable. How perfectly silly, therefore, for anyone who knows the value of promise to engage in the grave mistake of allowing his ability to be measured in the definite Here and Now! What good can such a measurement do you? If your grade is known, even though it be a fairly high grade, all your promise is shattered.

Just look at the countless near champions who have appeared in various lines of sports. The near champ may be a man of extraordinary ability; but just as soon as he is beaten by the champ, he has lost all his glamour, his limits are defined, and now he is a Little Man.

That's the cruel thing about sport. It goes entirely by batting averages, by scores, by win or lose. And when the game is over the stigma of incapacity, of inefficiency, of defeat is plastered on the loser.

In all of your activities in business or social life, steer clear of the showdown! Play your cards so that no one ever challenges you to a definite test of your powers. And never be so foolhardy as to be trapped by the temptation to show off, and led to compete in a contest where you must exert all of your powers in trying to win, and if you then lose let the whole world know how impotent are all your powers.

Just avoid the showdown, and in absence of any foundation for grading you, the world will grade you very high!

DEAR MR. MANGAN: *Never, never, never — NEVER have I enjoyed a book as much as I have enjoyed "The Knack of Selling Yourself." It's a peach, let me tell you. And I ought to know because I have read just about everything, past, present, and future!*

There's only one thing wrong with it: I didn't find it

soon enough. They should have fed it to me at eight years, and then sort of let me grow up with it. As it was, I read it for the first time about a year ago. And in trying to catch up since then I've raced through it exactly sixteen times.

Each time I read it, I get tangled up in something new and so exciting that I have to pop right up and chant that particular part to my love. "See, honey, what Mangan says? That's what I've been trying to say for months!"

How you did it, all between two covers, I don't know. How you packed so many interesting things in one book —but wait! I'll bet that's the secret! You've wound it up so tight with the things that really make us tick, that we never can quite exhaust it. It stays forever fresh and vital!

Well, you've probably heard this from a lot of other folks too, because by this time everybody I know of has read you. Only I've told so many other copywriters just what I think of "The Knack," that I guess it's about time I was telling you.

Thanks for writing it. It's a dandy—a Jim T. Mangan dandy! Yours, G. J.

DEAR JIM: I have just finished reading for the first time your wise and brilliant book, *The Knack of Selling Yourself,* and I want to congratulate you on a grand piece of work. I say "first" because it most certainly commands a second reading.

As you may know, I have read and admired almost everything you have ever published, but for useful service to the reader ~~and for strong,~~ lucid writing this, I think, is the best thing you have done.

Let me put it this way: This is the kind of book one feels honor bound to recommend to his friends. And. I don't know of a higher tribute to be paid a book than that.

It deserves a wide audience and a wide audience deserves to read it. Personally, I don't see how it can miss, given a good break in promotion and distribution.—P. H. E.

DEAR JIM: *Your book, "The Knack of Selling Yourself," contains more worthwhile, creative material than one finds in most expensive correspondence courses of study. It is a book employers should buy in quantities for use in their organizations. It is alive, colorful, informative and inspiring. It is a book to be read and re-read. Even I, hardened by years of reading so-called inspirational books, find it fresh and invigorating. I started to read it as a duty. Now I read it with genuine pleasure. It expresses the spirit of youth. Many a reader will find it an Open Sesame into a new world of success. You have reason to be proud of your new book.—T. D.*

CPSIA information can be obtained at www.ICGtesting.com
Printed in the USA
BVOW03s1420131014

370602BV00031B/632/P